DISCARD

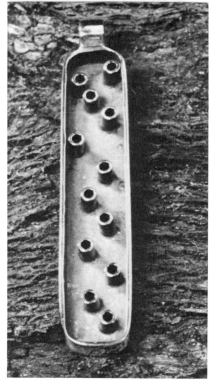

make your own
RINGS & OTHER THINGS:
working with silver

29389

OAKTON COMMUNITY COLLEGE
LEARNING RESOURCE CENTER
7900 N. Nagle Avenue
Morton Grove, Illinois 60053

DISCARD

BY ELSIE B. GINNETT

Photographs by Jacqueline A. Rose

STERLING
PUBLISHING CO., INC. NEW YORK
Oak Tree Press Co., Ltd.
London & Sydney

OTHER BOOKS OF INTEREST

Family Book of Crafts
Practical Encyclopedia of Crafts

LITTLE CRAFT BOOK SERIES

Aluminum and Copper Tooling
Appliqué and Reverse Appliqué
Balsa Wood Modelling
Bargello Stitchery
Beads Plus Macramé
Beauty Recipes from Natural Foods
Big-Knot Macramé
Candle-Making
Cellophane Creations
Ceramics by Slab
Coloring Papers
Corn-Husk Crafts
Corrugated Carton Crafting
Costumes from Crepe Paper
Crafting with Nature's Materials
Creating Silver Jewelry with Beads
Creating with Beads

Creating with Burlap
Creating with Flexible Foam
Creative Lace-Making with Thread and Yarn
Cross Stitchery
Curling, Coiling and Quilling
Decoupage—Simple and Sophisticated
Embossing of Metal (Repoussage)
Enamel without Heat
Felt Crafting
Finger Weaving: Indian Braiding
Flower Pressing
Folding Table Napkins
Greeting Cards You Can Make
Hooked and Knotted Rugs
Horseshoe-Nail Crafting
How to Add Designer Touches to Your Wardrobe
Ideas for Collage

Junk Sculpture
Lacquer and Crackle
Leathercrafting
Macramé
Make Your Own Elegant Jewelry
Make Your Own Rings and Other Things
Making Paper Flowers
Making Picture Frames
Making Shell Flowers
Masks
Metal and Wire Sculpture
Model Boat Building
Monster Masks
Mosaics with Natural Stones
Nail Sculpture
Needlepoint Simplified
Off-Loom Weaving

Organic Jewelry You Can Make
Patchwork and Other Quilting
Pictures without a Camera
Potato Printing
Puppet-Making
Repoussage
Scissorscraft
Scrimshaw
Sculpturing with Wax
Sewing without a Pattern
Starting with Stained Glass
Stone Grinding and Polishing
String Things You Can Create
Tissue Paper Creations
Tole Painting
Trapunto: Decorative Quilting
Whittling and Wood Carving

Second Printing, 1974

Copyright © 1974 by Sterling Publishing Co., Inc.
419 Park Avenue South, New York, N.Y. 10016
British edition published by Oak Tree Press Co., Ltd., Nassau, Bahamas
Distributed in Australia and New Zealand by Oak Tree Press Co., Ltd.,
P.O. Box J34, Brickfield Hill, Sydney 2000, N.S.W.
Distributed in the United Kingdom and elsewhere in the British Commonwealth
by Ward Lock Ltd., 116 Baker Street, London W 1
Manufactured in the United States of America
All rights reserved
Library of Congress Catalog Card No.: 73-83443
Sterling ISBN 0-8069-5270-9 Trade   Oak Tree 7061-2457-X
5271-7 Library

CONTENTS

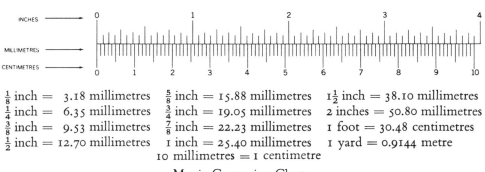

$\frac{1}{8}$ inch = 3.18 millimetres $\frac{5}{8}$ inch = 15.88 millimetres $1\frac{1}{2}$ inch = 38.10 millimetres

$\frac{1}{4}$ inch = 6.35 millimetres $\frac{3}{4}$ inch = 19.05 millimetres   2 inches = 50.80 millimetres

$\frac{3}{8}$ inch = 9.53 millimetres $\frac{7}{8}$ inch = 22.23 millimetres   1 foot = 30.48 centimetres

$\frac{1}{2}$ inch = 12.70 millimetres   1 inch = 25.40 millimetres   1 yard = 0.9144 metre

10 millimetres = 1 centimetre

Metric Conversion Chart

INTRODUCTION

Working with silver is not difficult. The techniques are easily mastered and the possibilities for expression of your own originality make it a fascinating hobby. The author assumes that the users of this book are untutored in silver-working, but have always longed to "do something." The directions are simply stated and the photographs, taken during actual teaching sessions by the author, are aimed at illustrating the text.

The projects in the book require the most simple materials and designs. The articles for which detailed directions are given are merely stepping stones to an endless variety of jewelry and related items. For example, you can also apply the techniques you use to make the most simple ring to the most complex pendant or belt buckle.

Realizing that any hobby can become quite expensive, the author has selected designs which require a minimum of materials. The list of essential tools has been compiled so as to include only those most necessary for the beginning hobbyist. With proper use and care, these implements will last many years.

You can purchase any tools and materials you need (including the silver) from metal supply houses or craft or hobby suppliers who carry silversmithing equipment. Also, lapidary shops sometimes carry silversmithing equipment.

Silver is sized by gauges—the higher the gauge number, the finer or thinner the silver. Hence, 24-gauge silver sheet is thinner than 18-gauge. See Illus. 1 for a chart of actual thicknesses of silver gauges.

The designs in this book are only suggestions. The thrill of using your own ideas and creating new patterns is what makes any artistic effort worthwhile. Do not be afraid to experiment—let yourself go!

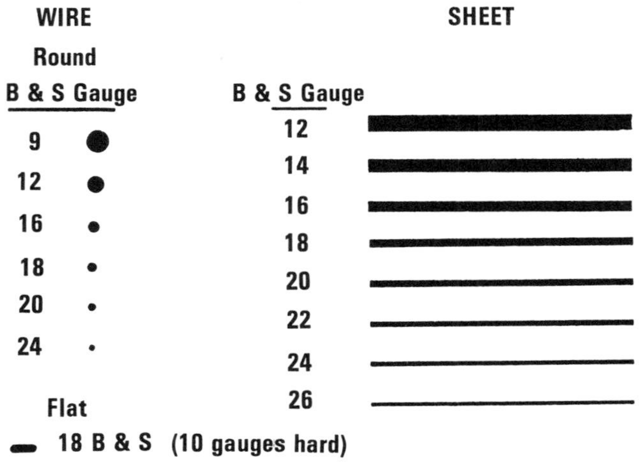

WIRE

Round

B & S Gauge

9 ●
12 ●
16 ●
18 •
20 •
24 •

Flat

➖ **18 B & S (10 gauges hard)**

SHEET

B & S Gauge

12
14
16
18
20
22
24
26

Illus. 1. Actual thicknesses of silver gauges for silver wire and sheet silver.

BASIC OVERLAY RING

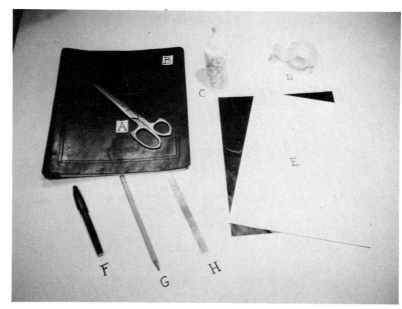

Illus. 2. Design equipment.

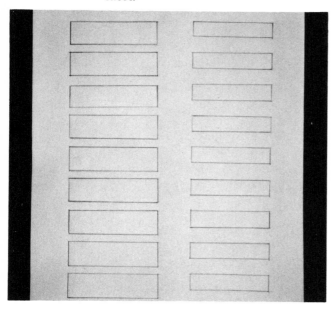

Illus. 3 (below). Divide a sheet of unlined paper into various ring widths for a design sheet.

How to Begin

DESIGN EQUIPMENT (Illus. 2)
A: scissors
B: notebook with unlined paper
C: white liquid glue (Elmer's)
D: cellophane tape
E: construction paper (light and dark)
F: felt pen (black, fine tip)
G: soft drawing pencil
H: metal ruler

To begin your first silver ring, divide a sheet of unlined paper into ring widths as shown in Illus. 3. Beginning at the top of the sheet, start to fill in all of the ring widths (Illus. 4). Doodle, make crosses, circles, squares, rec-

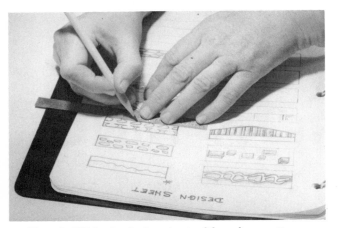

Illus. 4. Fill in the design sheet with various patterns.

Step 1: basic band

Step 2: overlay

Step 3: completed pattern

Illus. 5. Pattern for the basic overlay ring.

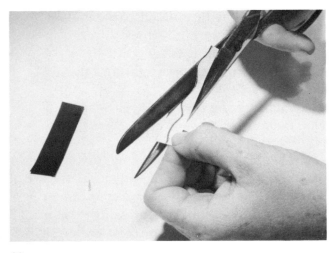

tangles, straight lines, squiggly lines, and so on. Vary the size of the designs. Try to arrange them so they are attractive and pleasing to your eye. Find a little pattern that satisfies you and repeat it several times in one ring width.

When you have filled all of the spaces on the design sheet, go back over them. Blacken some parts out with a pencil, shade others. Think of some of the patterns as being holes or absence of material, others as being raised.

For this chapter follow the design in Illus. 5, which has been divided into the three steps necessary for pattern construction.

Step 1: Cut a strip of dark construction paper 1 inch wide. Wrap it around the desired ring finger and cellophane tape it in place. Bend the finger. If the paper feels sharp and as though it would cut, the band is too wide. Keep trimming it to narrower widths until it feels comfortable.

To find the proper ring size, place the pattern for the basic band over the knuckle of the ring finger. It should be snug but should slide on and off without forcing. Mark the size as

Illus. 6 (above). Mark the proper size on the strip of construction paper.

Illus. 7 (left). Cut out the overlay design.

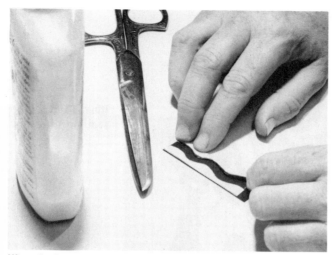

Illus. 8. Glue the two pieces of the overlay to the basic band.

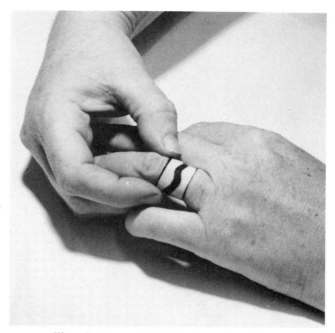

Illus. 9. Try on the finished mock-up ring.

shown in Illus. 6. Cut off the excess, leaving about $\frac{1}{4}$ inch beyond the mark to allow a strip for glueing. Now that you have determined the proper length and width for the band, trace and cut out a duplicate of it (minus the glue strip) for the final pattern.

Step 2: The overlay design for this particular ring, although as long, is not as wide as the basic band (Step 1). Draw the design on white construction paper. Cut it out as shown in Illus. 7. Make a copy of the overlay design for the final pattern. *Do not cut the copy in half yet.*

Step 3: The reason for the narrow overlay band becomes clear at this point. Glue the two pieces of the white overlay band to the outside edges of the basic band. See Illus. 8. Observe that the narrow overlay band, when cut in two and spread apart, makes a wide, dark middle strip. If you want a narrower center strip, increase the width of the overlay.

Make the mock-up round and glue it. This gives you a visual example of the completed ring. Think of the dark strip down the center as being an oxidized area—that is, treated with liver of sulphur, or its commercial equivalent, to turn it black. The white strips represent the areas which will be highly polished. See Illus. 9. Try on the mock-up ring, look at it, analyze

it. Does it look well on your hand? Is it too wide? Too narrow? Adjust the ring to fit your needs, and you are ready to proceed with its production.

GENERAL TOOL IDENTIFICATION
(Illus. 10)

A: saw blades, size 2/0
B: jeweller's saw, 3-inch
C: polished steel block
D: C-clamp, 3-inch
E: bench pin, homemade
F: ring mandrel
G: three needle files, 3-inch, all medium: triangular, half round, round
H: metal ruler
I: scribe
J: three pliers, $4\frac{1}{2}$-inch: round-nose, flat-nose, long-nose flat
K: C-clamp, 1-inch
L: jeweller's shears, straight-edged
M: bench vice
N: hammer with one plastic end, one metal end

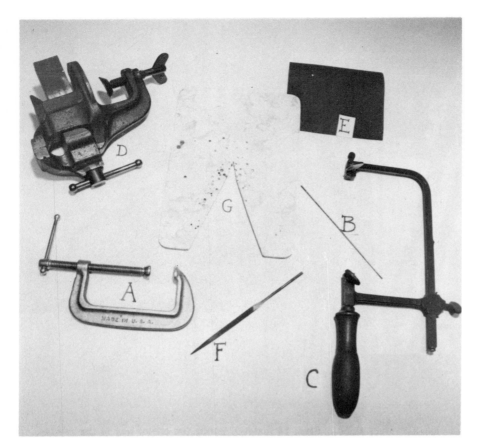

Illus. 15. Materials and tools for sawing and filing.

Sawing and Filing the Design

MATERIALS AND TOOLS (Illus. 15)

A: one 3-inch C-clamp
B: saw blades, size 2/0
C: one jeweller's saw, 3-inch (see Illus. 16)
D: bench vice
E: one sheet fine emery paper
F: half round needle file
G: bench pin

Sawing

The jeweller's saw has a rather fragile appearance that is misleading. It is a powerful and sturdy tool, which, if used properly, is capable of cutting the hardest of metals. Since this saw cuts only on the downward stroke, you must always set the blade so the teeth face *out* from the frame, and *down* towards the handle.

Loosen the wing nuts at each end of the jeweller's saw frame. Fasten the blade in the top holder first. Place the tip of the frame against the edge of the table, while holding it by the handle with your left hand. Push firmly against the table until the frame bends slightly and fasten the blade in the bottom holder. Fastened properly, the blade should make a musical ping when you strum it with your thumb.

Now, fasten the bench pin to the work bench with the 3-inch C-clamp. To judge the correct position accurately, let your right arm hang loosely at your side. Bend your arm at the elbow and raise your hand until it touches the edge of the table. You should center the V in the bench pin here. Mount the vice on the right of the bench pin. (Reverse this procedure if you are left-handed.) See Illus. 17.

Hold the jeweller's saw in a vertical position (see Illus. 18). As mentioned earlier, this saw cuts only on the downward stroke, so its

14

Illus. 16. Jeweller's saw and saw blade.

motion is up and down and not forward as with a hand saw. You pull it downwards, gently slide it up, and pull it downwards again. Frequent breakage of saw blades usually means you have tilted the saw forward or that you have forced or rushed the sawing. Take your time—try to make the motions as smooth as possible.

Place the 18-gauge silver on the bench pin, scribed side up. Put the saw blade up against the beginning of the scribe mark. Place the first and second fingers of your left hand, one on

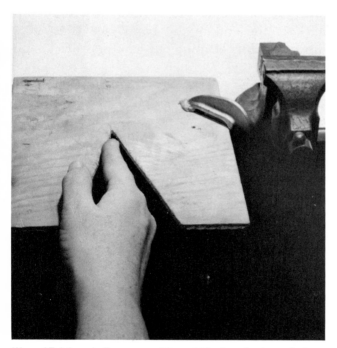

Illus. 17 (above). Proper position of the bench pin and vice.

Illus. 18 (right). The proper grip of the jeweller's saw is in a vertical position.

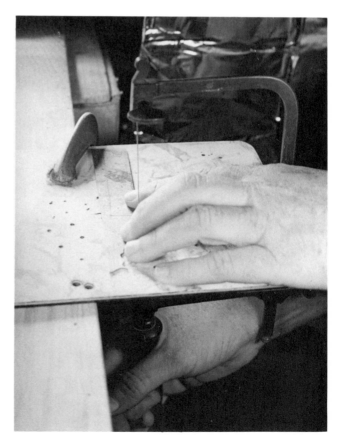

Illus. 19. Hold your fingers and the silver as shown here when sawing out the basic band.

each side of the blade, on the silver (see Illus. 19). Hold the silver down firmly and tightly against the bench pin. If at any time while sawing the silver slaps against the board, you are holding it too loosely.

On the first try, do not saw on the mark but alongside it. Stay as close as possible, but do not permit the saw to cross over the line. You can control the direction of the cut by one of two methods: either move your hand to change the direction of the saw or move the silver right or left. The choice is up to you.

Saw past the corner of the outline by about $\frac{1}{16}$ inch. When you reach this point, relax—let the saw coast with the up-and-down movement. Very gently, a little at a time, turn the near end of the silver towards your right hand until the saw blade is parallel to the scribe mark at the end of the band (see Illus. 20). Finish the cut, keeping the saw parallel to the line.

Cut out the overlay scribed on the piece of 22-gauge silver in the same manner, with one exception: saw the wavy center line first (see

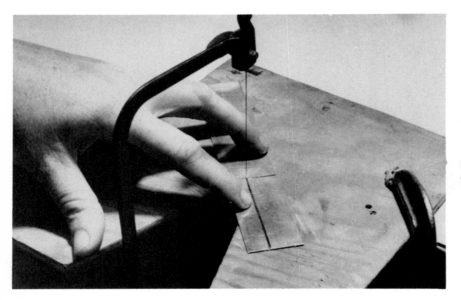

Illus. 20. To turn the corner, gently turn the silver towards your right hand until the saw blade is parallel with the scribe mark.

Illus. 21. Saw the wavy center line of the overlay first.

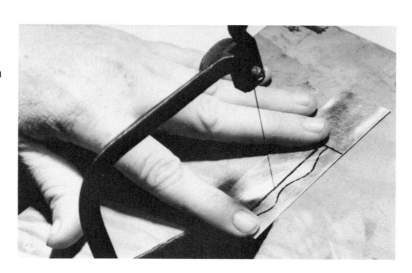

Illus. 22. After you have sawed the wavy line, then saw the outline of the overlay.

Illus. 23 (below). Place the sawed overlay piece into the bench vice.

Illus. 21). This time you must saw *exactly* on the line. When you reach $\frac{1}{16}$ inch beyond the scribed end of the band, back the saw out of the cut by pulling gently and moving the saw up and down. Be sure to hold the silver down firmly so that you do not break the saw blade.

Saw the long outline mark next (Illus. 22). Turn the corner as described earlier. Cut the end of the band about $\frac{1}{16}$ inch longer than the mark.

Filing

With all your pieces cut out, you are now ready to file. Place the overlay design, one

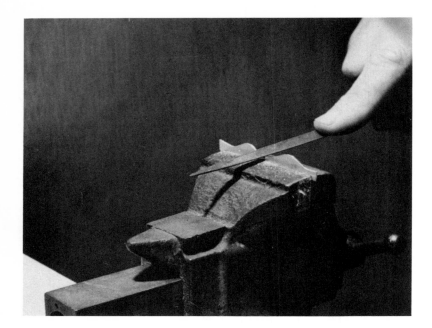

Illus. 24. The proper way to hold the file.

piece at a time, in the vice as shown in Illus. 23. Hold the file in your right hand on a level plane. It is important that you do not allow the file to dip at the tip or the handle end. Turn the round side of the file down towards the silver. Use the whole cutting surface of the file and follow the wavy surface of the design. File with a movement which is both forward

Illus. 25. Sweep the filings into a small box and save them for later use.

Illus. 26. Use medium emery paper to remove file marks from the overlay pieces.

Illus. 27. Clean all surfaces you plan to solder with fine emery paper.

and to the side, until you have removed all of the saw marks. Repeat this on both pieces of the overlay design.

Keep a small box handy in your work area so that you may sweep up filings and save them for later use (see Illus. 25).

Next, use a small piece of medium emery paper rolled into a tube in the manner pictured in Illus. 26. Remove all the file marks on both overlay pieces.

It is important that all of the surfaces that you plan to solder are clean—that is, free of dirt, oxides, and oil from fingers. You may clean the pieces by rubbing the surfaces shiny with fine emery paper. Once cleaned, do not touch the surfaces to be soldered with your fingers; use tweezers whenever possible (see Illus. 27).

Soldering

IDENTIFICATION OF SOLDERING TOOLS (Illus. 28)

A: hard, medium and easy solder with box for storage
B: self pickling flux
C: water-color brush

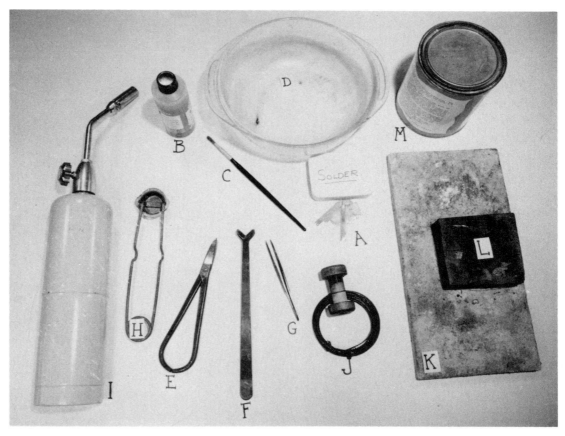

Illus. 28. Identification of soldering tools.

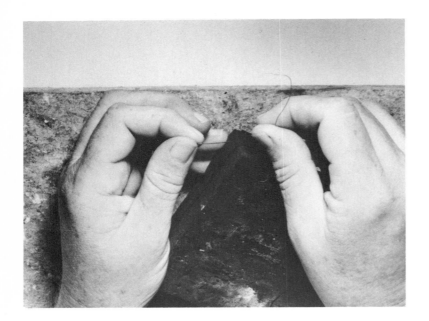

Illus. 29. Binding the charcoal block.

D: pickling pan (copper or oven-proof glass)
E: jeweller's shears (same as L in Illus. 10)
F: copper tongs
G: tweezers (soldering tweezers or an old pair of household tweezers)
H: lighter for torch (kitchen matches will do)
I: propane torch (disposable cylinder)

J: binding or stove wire (fine and heavy)
K: asbestos pad
L: 3-inch charcoal block
M: pickling compound (commercial product recommended as it is safer than sulphuric acid)

Illus. 30. Mark the solder for easy identification, and store it in a small box.

POINTS OF INTEREST IN SOLDERING:
Sterling silver melts at 1,640°F (893°C)
Hard solder melts at 1,475°F (802°C)
Medium solder melts at 1,390°F (756°C)
Easy solder melts at 1,325°F (718°C)

Before proceeding further, take the time to bind the edge of the charcoal block with some binding wire. This little trick prolongs the block's usefulness considerably and prevents it from splitting apart through repeated use (see Illus. 29).

Prepare to Solder

The strips of hard, medium and easy solder all look the same to anyone who is not an expert. So, take no chances. Mark each piece with a scribe as you take it from the envelope. For example, scratch the letter "H" all the way up the center of the hard solder strip. Then, no matter how small the last scrap, it will still be easy to identify. A small lozenge or cigarette box is ideal for solder storage. See Illus. 30.

Clean the piece of hard solder on both sides of one end with emery paper as described on page 19. Make a number of narrow cuts with the jeweller's shears (about ½ inch long) up the length of the solder. The strips will curl as you cut. Straighten them out by rubbing on the side opposite the curl with the jeweller's shears. To prevent the solder squares from flying as you cut them, hold the solder in your left hand. Place the index finger of that hand across the end of the solder where you have made the ½-inch cuts. Hold the solder over the lid of the solder box and, with the shears, cut across the width of the strips so you form little squares about $\frac{1}{16}$ inch (see Illus. 31).

You must first thoroughly flux all surfaces (solder and silver) you plan to join together. Flux is a borax mixture which helps prevent oxides and permits the smooth flow of the solder as it melts and becomes liquid. You may apply flux with a brush or hold the pieces of silver or solder with tweezers and dip them in the flux bottle (see Illus. 32).

Illus. 31. Cut the solder into little squares for use.

Illus. 32. Apply flux with a brush to the band.

After you have fluxed the basic band, place it on the charcoal block with the cleaned, fluxed side *up*. Now apply solder squares in one of two ways: with tweezers or with a flux brush. If using tweezers, dip each square in the flux as you place it on the band. If using the flux brush, you must moisten it for the application of each piece. Place solder under the overlay so it conforms to the wavy design, one piece at the crest of the wave and one at the ebb

(where the design narrows). Repeat this to the end of the band. Make sure there is one piece of solder directly in the center of each overlay piece at each end of the band. With the tweezers, place the overlay pieces, cleaned and fluxed side *down*, in position. There should be no solder pieces showing. If you discover any, push them underneath the edge of the overlay with tweezers.

It is only permissible to touch, with your fingers, any surface that you are not going to solder.

NOTE: *Oxide prevention.* Oxides are the result of heating the metal during the soldering or annealing (see page 26) processes. On prolonged soldering projects, it is possible to hold oxidation to a minimum by fluxing the entire object. Parts that are in direct contact with the charcoal block need not be fluxed as it offers its own protection against oxidation. If you heat the object to be soldered quickly and efficiently, the oxides will not have time to burn deeply into the silver.

From the coil of binding wire, cut six lengths, each ½ inch long. Bend each piece at about ⅓ its length into an L shape. Pin the ring to the

charcoal block with these wires. Use three on each side to be soldered (one on each end, one in the middle) (see Illus. 34). When this is finished, take a quick survey to make sure the ring parts are in proper alignment and make any adjustments necessary.

Illus. 34. Pin the ring to the charcoal block with L-shaped pieces of wire.

Torches

There are several kinds of torches available that you may use for soldering silver.

The propane torch in the illustrations in this book has a disposable cylinder, is economical, and is available in hardware departments or from mail-order suppliers. It has a clean, easily controlled flame.

You can also use a gas-air torch which utilizes a combination of gas and compressed air. The gas can be either manufactured illuminating gas, natural gas or propane. Air pressure is supplied by a foot bellows or by a motor-driven compressor.

Acetylene torches are portable, and although they are initially expensive to buy, the refill tanks are low in cost and readily available.

Another recommended torch unit uses a tank of oxygen and the natural gas that is normally supplied in homes. Many artists are using this set-up.

Following are some important facts to remember when deciding which flame you should use to solder (see Illus. 35): The flame shown in Illus. 35A is called a soft flame. You use this occasionally to dry flux on complicated soldering projects. Drying the flux this slowly (for a second or two) prevents it from bubbling and causing the solder to jump out of place. You can also use this flame, sometimes, to solder delicate parts together, such as two fine wires.

The flame shown in Illus. 35B is the correct flame for most soldering projects. Notice the sharp point in the middle of the flame. The tip of this point indicates the hottest area of the entire flame. The tip should always be near, but not touching, the surface of the object being soldered.

In Illus. 35C, the torch has been turned higher for illustration. When the hot tip disappears, the heat dissipates. You should

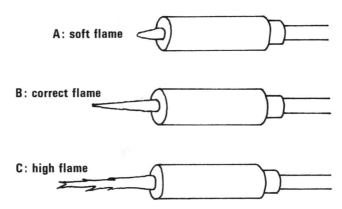

A: soft flame

B: correct flame

C: high flame

Illus. 35. Various flames on the propane torch.

not use this flame, as it will not heat as effectively and will cause unnecessary fire scale and oxides.

Soldering

Follow a pattern with the tip of the flame when soldering—a figure eight or, as the author has done on this ring, the letter "N." To make the N, for example, solder up one side, down the middle and up the other side. This technique helps to assure that you heat all parts of the item to be soldered uniformly. See Illus. 36.

When the solder reaches its liquid state and

Illus. 36. Follow a pattern when you solder to ensure that you heat all parts of the silver uniformly.

Illus. 37. Draw solder, by the heat of the flame, to specific areas of the ring.

begins to flow, it is a thin, bright, silvery line, and will probably appear first in the middle of the overlay. During this period (two or three seconds), you may draw solder by the heat of the flame to specific areas of the work (see Illus. 37). To ensure that the solder has completely melted under the overlay, run the torch up and down both outside edges of the ring. The correct approach to soldering is to

heat quickly and uniformly at all times, thus avoiding excess fire scale and oxides.

Now, using tweezers, remove the ring from the charcoal block and quench it in water. Then, pickle it.

Pickling

Pickling is a cleansing, conditioning process. To mix a pickling solution, carefully follow the directions on the container of solution which you have bought. Sparex #2 is one commercial pickling solution. It is granular and easy to measure. You mix it with water to use it.

You can make your own pickling solution by adding one part sulphuric acid to 10 parts water. *You must add the acid to the water*, or the mixture will explode. Sulphuric acid, however, is dangerous—if spilled, it eats holes in clothes, floors, and so on. To neutralize it on your skin, rinse the area with cold water and apply a paste of baking soda to the area.

You may stir pickle with anything made of oven-proof glass, stainless steel or copper. Note that the smallest bit of iron in the solution causes any silver placed in it to discolor.

Place the pickle pan on the stove or a hot plate. Turn it on *low*. The solution should

Illus. 38. Place the pickle pan on a stove or hot plate, and, with copper tongs, place the ring in the simmering solution.

Illus. 39. Leave the ring in the pickle solution until it is frosty white.

simmer, but not boil. Using copper tongs, place the ring in the pickle. When all signs of oxidation have disappeared and the silver is frosty white, remove the ring and rinse it thoroughly in cold water.

Rinse the pickle pan in cold water and dust it with baking soda before storing it away. This will neutralize any acid remaining in it after use.

If you plan to store pickle between projects, keep it in a well labelled glass jar. Be sure it is out of the reach of children, but never above your own eye level.

CAUTION: Always do pickling in a well ventilated room. Because you should always consider the solution *acid,* *never* stand directly over the pan while it is steaming, as the fumes can be potent. If pickle should spatter on your skin, you may neutralize it by running cold water over the area. If irritation persists, apply a paste of baking soda mixed with water to the area.

Trim, with the saw and file, the ends of the ring length so they are square (Illus. 40). Solder will not fill in gaps caused by imperfect workmanship.

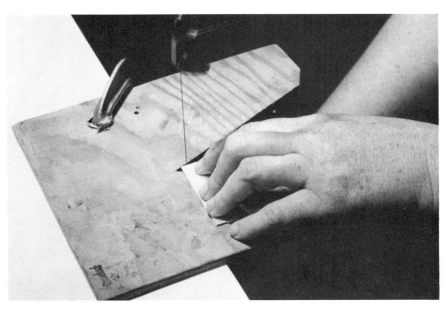

Illus. 40. Trim the ends of the ring length so they are square.

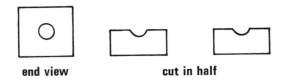

end view   cut in half

Illus. 41. How to make polishing blocks.

Annealing

In annealing you heat the silver until it begins to turn a dull red, then immediately quench it in cold water or pickle. When silver is pounded or stretched, it hardens. You may return it to its softer, more workable state by annealing.

Anneal the ring length.

Making Polishing and Forming Blocks

To make polishing blocks, use two 5-inch lengths of 4 × 4 wood. Sometimes, you may find these in the scrap pile of a new building site or a lumber yard. Drill a hole through the middle of each piece, then saw the blocks in half (see Illus. 41). Smooth each half with sandpaper. Cover two halves with moleskin (see page 30) across the top and down into the groove. With a felt-tip marking pen, label the end of one block TRIPOLI and the other ROUGE (these terms will be discussed further on page 30). Set these aside. You will use them later in polishing. Use another half, as is, as the forming block.

Place one end of the ring length across the groove in the forming block. Hold the dowel in position as shown in Illus. 42, and strike it (not the silver) with the hammer. Move to the other end of the silver and repeat. Frequently, switch the ring length end for end. Continue this procedure, gradually working towards the middle until the length is rounded.

Try the ring on for size. If it is too large, you may trim *small* sections off each end in the following manner: Place the ring in the bench vice with the joint on top as in Illus. 43. Lay the saw blade on top of the mark scribed for the cut. Guide the blade with your index finger to prevent it from slipping. Gently move the saw back and forth until the cut is complete. Repeat on the opposite side. File the ends to ensure a smooth, close-fitting joint.

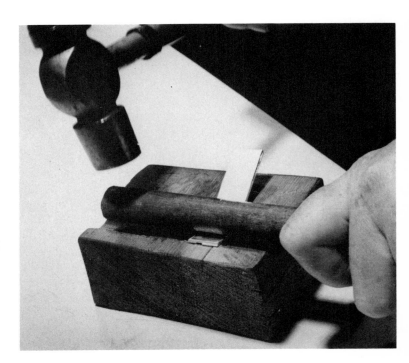

Illus. 42. Bend the ring length in the forming block using a dowel and hammer.

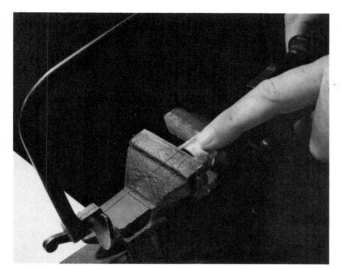

Illus. 43. Trim the ring in the bench vice if it is too big.

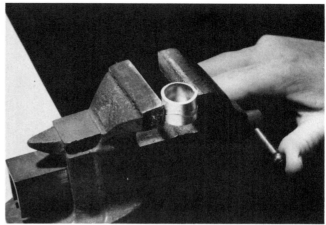

Illus. 44. You may bend the ring ends together in the bench vice if you have trouble in the forming block.

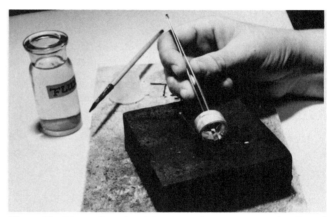

Illus. 45. Place fluxed solder directly on top of the fluxed joint.

Illus. 46. To solder the ring joint, move the heat in a pattern until the solder begins to melt. Then, concentrate the heat on the joint.

Round the ring again and try it on. It should be snug, for polishing enlarges it slightly.

Anneal and pickle the ring again, using the method previously described. In a heavy-gauge ring such as this, it may be difficult to bend the ring ends together using only your fingers or the forming block. If such is the case, you may insert the ring in the bench vice, as shown in Illus. 44, and bend one side at a time until both ends are flush. (It would be wise to line the jaws of the bench vice with two small pieces of moleskin to avoid marring the silver.) This will flatten the ring, but it is not essential that it be perfectly round at this time. Run the tip of one finger across the joint. If you feel any ridges, the ends are not flush. Keep bending until the ridges disappear.

Clean the ring joint inside and out with emery. Do the same to both sides of one end of the *medium* solder. Cut a thin strip of solder long enough to cover the ring joint from one edge to the other. Flux the solder.

With tweezers, place the ring on the charcoal block, joint side *down*. Flux the joint and place the strip of fluxed solder inside, directly on top of the joint (see Illus. 45).

Heat the ring in a pattern as described earlier (see page 23). Move the heat across the top, down the right edge, inside the bottom and up the left edge (see Illus. 46). Repeat this

Illus. 47. Pickle the ring.

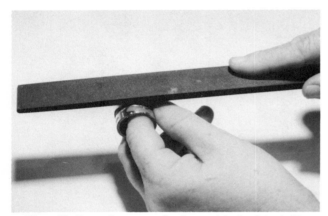

Illus. 48. Smooth any rough edges with the 6-inch file.

pattern until the solder begins to melt. Only then concentrate the heat on the solder.

Pickle and rinse the ring (Illus. 47). Inspect the ring closely to see if the joint is properly soldered. Re-solder where necessary.

If the soldering turned out well, very little filing is necessary. If, however, there are rough, uneven spots, you may smoothe them out with the 6-inch file, as shown in Illus. 48. Let the file follow the contour of the ring. Hold the file level and do not allow it to dip on one side or the other. When you have finished, go over the area with the fine, half round, 6-inch file using the same method.

Use the rounded side of the needle file to clean the solder bits from the inside of the ring joint (see Illus. 49). Use the whole length of the cutting edge in a movement that is both forward and to the side. Do not allow the file to dip at either end.

Now, you may round the ring on the mandrel as shown in Illus. 50. Notice that a small square of moleskin has been applied to the plastic end of the hammer to avoid marring the ring. Push the ring as far up on the mandrel as possible. Strike the ring on the high side, completely around its circumference. Reverse the ring and repeat this operation on the other edge. Keep forcing the ring as high on the mandrel as it will go. Follow this procedure until the ring is perfectly round.

To file the outside edges of the ring evenly, lay the ring on the flat 6-inch file and move it back and forth across the file's entire cutting surface (see Illus. 51). Turn the ring several times during the process. When both edges of the ring are smooth, repeat the same steps using the 6-inch half round fine file.

Illus. 49. Clean bits of solder from the inside of the ring joint with the rounded side of the needle file.

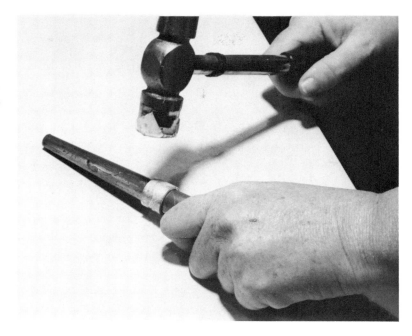

Illus. 50. Round the ring on the mandrel. Be sure to place a piece of moleskin on the head of the hammer to avoid marring the silver.

Hand Polishing

Now you are ready to polish your ring. The purpose of polishing is to wear away the surface of the metal to the depth of the deepest blemish—that is, fire scales and scratches. Fire scales, as well as fire flakes and fire coat, are common names for cupric or cuprous oxides—discolorations which appear on the surface of silver after it has been heated. Because pure silver, or fine silver, is too soft to work with, alloys are added to harden the silver (such silver is called sterling silver). Fire scale results when the base metal of the alloy added separates on the surface of the silver.

You can remove such blemishes by rubbing the surface of the metal first with emery sticks and then with felt buffs that have been charged with polishing compounds.

Illus. 51. File the outside edges of the ring on the flat 6-inch file.

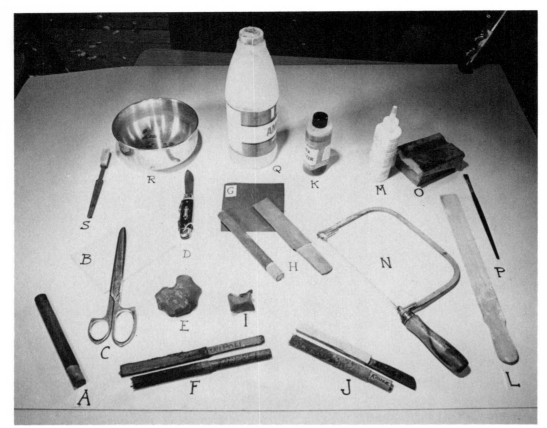

POLISHING EQUIPMENT (Illus. 52)

A: dowels, available in various sizes; dowel pictured is $\frac{1}{2}$ inch; use for polishing the inside surface of the ring

B: moleskin, a commercial product used in the care of the feet; a felt-like material, with an adhesive back, which you can easily cut to desired size and use to cover the dowels and paddles which are necessary in hand polishing

C: scissors, a sharp pair

D: sharp knife, use for shaping paddles

E: tripoli, a coarse polishing compound which you use in the primary polishing steps; it actually cuts away the surface of the silver and removes scratches and fire scale; take care not to destroy the sharpness of the design when using this polishing agent; keep the tripoli cake and the tripoli charged buffs apart from the other polishing materials; a plastic bag is ideal for storage

F: felt buffs: one dowel and one paddle covered with moleskin and charged with tripoli; notice that each has TRIPOLI written on the handle to distinguish them from ROUGE (see J)

G: emery paper: you may glue various grades to paddles and dowels; excellent for clean-up work on rings before final polishing

H: emery dowel and paddle

I: jeweller's rouge, a fine polishing agent composed of red iron oxide with a wax base; use to obtain a final high polish on silver

J: felt buffs, one dowel and one paddle covered with moleskin and charged with rouge; notice that each has ROUGE written on the handle; keep buffs in a separate plastic bag

K: liver of sulphur (or commercial equivalent), which, after diluting in water, you paint on silver in selected areas to cause them to oxidize (turn dark); you may use a commercial equivalent as it comes from the bottle

L: paint paddle, usually obtainable in a paint store free of charge; easily cut to any shape

M: white liquid glue, to attach emery paper to polishing sticks and dowels

N: coping saw, to cut paint paddles into polishing sticks of desired lengths and widths

O: polishing blocks, with the top surface of each block covered with moleskin; mark one block TRIPOLI and the other ROUGE; use to hold the ring while applying the final polishing

P: water-color brush, small, to apply oxidizer to desired areas of project

Q: ammonia, mixed with detergent and warm water; use to clean tripoli or rouge from projects

R: scrub bowl to use for ammonia, detergent and warm water solution when scrubbing tripoli and rouge from projects

S: toothbrush, a soft one, for the above process

Illus. 53. Clean the inside of the ring with the emery dowel.

Illus. 54. Clean the outside of the ring with the emery paddle.

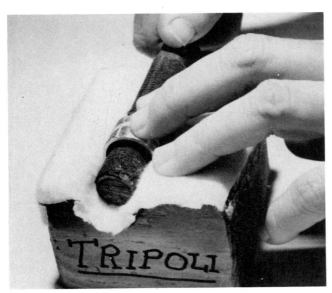

Illus. 55. Polish the inside of the ring with the tripoli dowel.

Steps in Hand Polishing

For *Step 1*, you need:

2 emery dowels, one medium, one fine

Using the forming block for support, clean the entire surface of the ring with the medium emery stick (dowel). You can remove most deep scratches and surface blemishes with this step. Repeat the above, using the fine emery stick until you achieve a fine matt surface.

31

Illus. 56. Polish the outside of the ring with the tripoli buff.

For *Step 2*, you need:
    1 tripoli polishing block
    1 buff (dowel)
    1 buff (paddle)
    1 tripoli cake

Using the tripoli polishing block for support, buff the inside and outside surfaces of the ring. Use as much pressure as possible. This process actually moves the surface of the silver, filling in fine scratches and producing a soft lustrous finish.

Step 3: Mix of one capful of ammonia and one capful of detergent in warm water. Scrub the ring with a soft brush, as in Illus. 57, until you have removed all traces of tripoli compound. At this point, fire flake—small shadows on the surface of the metal—begins to appear. If not completely removed, these little areas tarnish quickly and spoil the appearance of the ring. To remove fire flake, repeat the polishing steps from the fine emery stick to the tripoli buffs. Pressure with the tripoli buffs shortens the process. Always scrub the silver object with the ammonia solution before proceeding to the next step.

Place a lump of liver of sulphur, the size of a small coin, in a small bottle (a spice or vitamin bottle will do). Fill the bottle 4/5 full with cold water. Put the cap on and shake until the liver of sulphur is dissolved. (You may use the

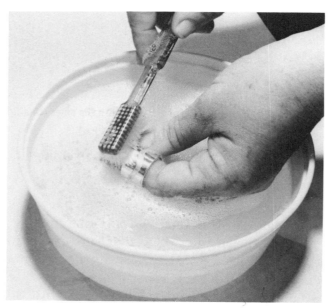

Illus. 57. Scrub the ring in a solution of ammonia and detergent.

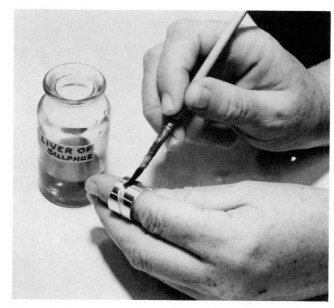

Illus. 58. Paint the area you want oxidized with liver of sulphur.

commercial equivalent of liver of sulphur as it comes from the bottle.)

Paint the middle strip of the ring with this solution using a water-color brush (see Illus. 58). Let it stand for a few minutes. When the area is dark enough, dry the ring thoroughly with a paper towel.

NOTE: Some craftsmen prefer to heat these solutions to obtain a darker oxide. However, if you do this, be prepared for the smell, which is very pungent.

For *Step 4* you need:

    1 rouge polishing block
    1 buff (dowel)
    1 buff (paddle)
    1 rouge cake

With this step, the ring gains dimension and depth. Rouge is a very fine polishing agent that gives silver its highest shine. Follow the directions previously described in the use of tripoli (see page 32). Lightly brush the ring in the solution used in Illus. 57 and dry it with a paper towel.

Your finished project should look like Illus. 60.

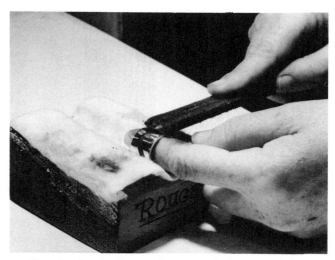

Illus. 59. Do the final polishing with the rouge buff.

Illus. 60 (below). Finished basic overlay ring.

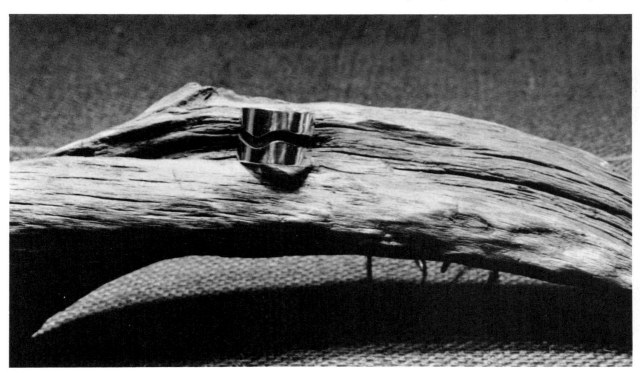

TEXTURED OVERLAY RINGS

Texturing is used in silversmithing to break up the flat surfaces of a project in order to reflect light and bring out the design.

The two rings in Illus. 61 and 62 require much more patience and skill in soldering, but they are actually simple variations of the ring in Illus. 60. Use the overlay pattern (Step 2) shown in Illus. 5 for the wavy strips used on these rings.

Take care in soldering these little strips. Be

Illus. 62. Another textured adaptation of the basic overlay ring has six stripes.

Illus. 61. This textured ring is merely a variation of the basic overlay ring in Illus. 60.

very sure that you firmly fasten the work to the charcoal block and that you securely solder all parts of the strips to the basic band before you round the ring. If you do not do this, the strips will distort when bent.

Drilling

Groupings of drill and burr holes of assorted sizes can create some interesting effects. Place the ring part to be drilled on the hardwood or steel block and make a "starter" mark with a punch and hammer. This mark keeps the drill from skidding and leaving unwanted scars on the surface of the silver. Then fasten the ring

Illus. 63. Examples of drill and burr texturing.

part to the bench pin with a small C-clamp and drill (see Illus. 63).

You may place a burr in an already-drilled hole to enlarge it.

Nail-Set Texturing

This is a simple and inexpensive way of texturing. You must remember, however, that when you hammer silver, you stretch and harden it. Therefore, you should do most texturing *before* you assemble the parts for soldering. You must then anneal the textured piece (see page 26).

The ring in Illus. 64, a very simple one, consists of two parts: the basic band and the overlay (see Illus. 65). The pattern illustrated shows some textured areas as well as dark ovals which you will cut out.

Cut out and fit the pattern and construct a mock-up ring, as shown in Illus. 66. When you are sure of a good fit, scribe the outline of the basic band on a piece of 18-gauge silver (as

Illus. 64. This handsome ring combines nail-set texturing and oval cut-outs.

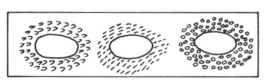

basic band with texturing

overlay

Illus. 65. Pattern for the textured ring in Illus. 64.

described on page 12) and saw it out. Scribe the ovals next.

You should place all projects you plan to texture on a hardwood or steel block. Then hold the nail set firmly against the silver and strike with a hammer, one blow per mark.

For this ring, place the basic band, scribed side up, on the polished steel block. Using a punch and hammer, strike a mark in the middle of each oval. Fasten the band to the bench pin, using a small C-clamp. Place the tip of the drill in the punch mark and drill a hole.

When you have completed drilling, remove the band from the C-clamp. Loosen the top clamp of the saw frame and pull the loose end of the saw blade through the drilled hole.

Fasten the saw blade again and saw in an arc towards the scribe mark. Take care to stay as close to the line as possible without allowing the saw to cross over it.

When you have cut out all of the ovals, place the basic band in the bench vice so the scribed marks are visible. Use the half round needle file and file the oval until the cut is even with the scribe mark. Roll a small piece of emery paper into a tube and remove the file marks from the inside of the ovals.

Scribe and saw out the overlay employing the techniques just used. Place the overlay on top of the basic band and lightly scribe the outline of the larger ovals. Then place the basic band on the steel block, scribed side up.

You may actually do texturing with any instrument which leaves an interesting mark. The author chose for this design a small screwdriver, a nail set and a small dappling punch. You may hold the nail set straight up and down or tilt it slightly. You may also vary the force of the blows from the hammer (see Illus. 67).

Illus. 67. Various examples of nail-set texturing.

Illus. 68. This textured ring has seven oval insets on the overlay band.

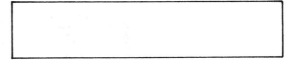

basic band

overlay with seven insets

Illus. 69. Pattern for the textured ring in Illus. 68.

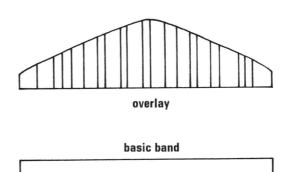

overlay

basic band

Illus. 70. Pattern for the filed textured ring in Illus. 71.

Texturing should cross slightly over the lightly scribed line. When you have completed this step, you are ready to solder the two parts together. Use the techniques for soldering you learned while making the first ring (see pages 23 to 25).

When you have rounded the ring and soldered the ring joint, file the edges. Taper the outside edges slightly to remove any uncomfortable sharpness.

Turn the half round, 6-inch file, round side down, and file the holes in the basic band to remove any sharp edges. Finish the ring following the procedures outlined on pages 26 to 33.

The ring in Illus. 68, similar to the one in Illus. 64, is smart and easily executed. It consists of nine parts: the basic band, the overlay, and seven oval insets (see the pattern in Illus. 69). Follow the procedures and techniques you used on the previous ring, with the following differences: use 22-gauge silver for the basic band and 18-gauge silver, which is heavier, for the overlay and insets.

Filing

You can do some very attractive forms of texturing with the three needle files shown in Illus. 10, item G.

Illus. 71. The texture on this ring was produced by filing.

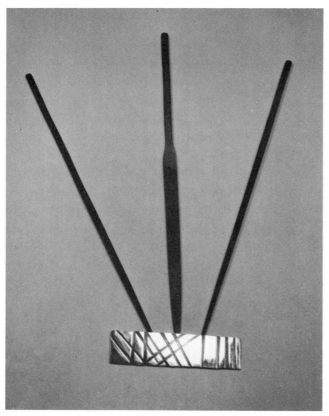

Illus. 72. Examples of filings.

The pattern for the ring in Illus. 71 has two parts: the basic band and the overlay (see Illus. 70). You should file this ring before soldering the overlay to the basic band.

Firmly fasten the item you want to file to the bench pin with a small C-clamp or hold it in the bench vice. Any line you decide to file should go all the way across the ring surface. Be careful not to allow the file to dip at either end (see Illus. 72).

After filing, complete the ring as you did the previous overlay rings.

Shot

Shot is the name given to little balls of silver which you can solder to a surface for texture. You can make shot from scrap silver or from uniform lengths cut from silver wire. Then heat the scraps on the charcoal block until they melt and form balls. Pickle the shot balls, and they are ready to use (see Illus. 73).

The ring in Illus. 74 is an example of shot used for texture.

Illus. 73 (above). You can use shot balls in many ways to texture your silver projects.

Illus. 74 (right). Shot was used for texturing this unusual ring.

TABLE RING

A table ring has a table or base to which you attach a ring band. The pattern in this case consists of four parts: the outside band, the inside design, the table to which they are fastened, the ring band (see Illus. 75).

Cut out the outside band from paper. Bend where indicated and glue. It is not necessary to have a perfect rectangle or absolute "squared" corners. When the glue is dry, use this as a pattern for the table. To do this, place the outside band on a piece of dark construction paper and trace round it with a pencil. Cut out the tracing on the outside of the pencil mark. Glue the two pieces together.

Then, cut out the inside design and bend where the pattern is marked. Fit this into the

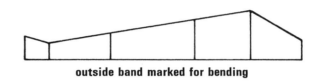

outside band marked for bending

Illus. 75. Pattern for the table ring.

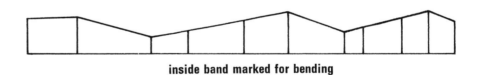

inside band marked for bending

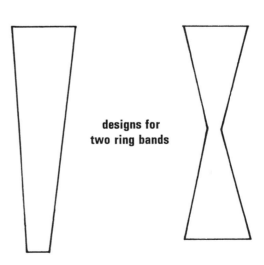

**designs for
two ring bands**

adaptable and you may use them over and over on different rings. When fitting the mock-up ring band, leave a gap of about $\frac{1}{8}$ inch between the ends of the band. Glue them to the table top this way.

When you are sure the mock-up is comfortable and of the right proportions, scribe round the outside band pattern on a piece of 18-gauge silver, and cut it out. When you have sawed the part out, file the two ends of the band carefully to ensure a square, snug fitting joint for soldering. Use the paper pattern as a guide and bend the outside band as shown in Illus. 77.

Using a small piece of emery paper, clean both sides of the joint to be soldered. Take care not to touch these areas with your fingers after cleaning. Then, bind the band, as shown in Illus. 78, with a piece of wire. This prevents the ends from spreading apart when heated.

Flux the entire piece and place it, joint *down*, on the charcoal block. Cut a thin strip of *hard* solder, just long enough to cover the width of the joint. Flux it and place it in position. Solder. Remember to follow a pattern

already-constructed part. When you are sure of the fit, lift this piece out, put a small amount of the glue on the bottom of the table and re-fit the piece. You may hold the parts together with a little piece of cellophane tape across the top until they dry.

Two possible patterns for ring bands are shown in Illus. 75 so you may choose the one most to your liking. Both bands are very

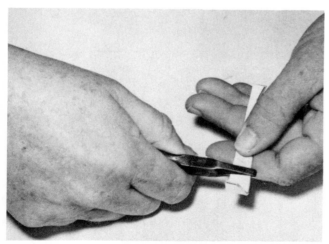

Illus. 77. Bend the outside band using the paper pattern as a guide.

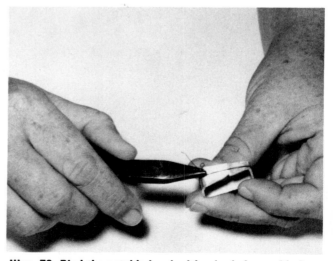

Illus. 78. Bind the outside band with wire before soldering.

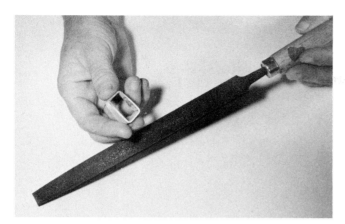

Illus. 79. File the bottom of the outside band on the flat 6-inch file.

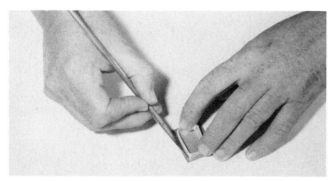

Illus. 80. Scribe the outline of the soldered band on a piece of 22-gauge silver for the table.

with the torch while soldering so all parts of the band will be equally hot. If you do not do this properly, the solder will run to one side of the joint only.

Quench the band in water. Remove the binding wire. The band should require little or no filing if soldered properly. Be very sure there are no little pieces of the binding wire left on the band, as iron discolors silver if the two are pickled together. Rinse in cold water and dry. Place the band, bottom *down*, on the flat 6-inch file and file until smooth and uniform (see Illus. 79).

Use the soldered band as a guide and scribe its outline on a piece of 22-gauge silver (see Illus. 80). Be sure to saw on the outside edge of scribe mark. Do not file at this time, but clean the side of the table to be soldered with emery paper.

Use four L-shaped wires to pin the two pieces

to the charcoal block. Flux. Place snippets of *hard* solder against the side of the band all around as shown in Illus. 81.

Use a piece of 26-gauge silver for the inside design and follow the same procedures you used in sawing the outside band. File the ends and finish with emery paper. Use as a guide the paper pattern and bend the design, starting at the inside. Some small adjustments may be necessary to ensure a proper fit. File the bottom of the design as you did the outside band.

Illus. 81. Solder placement against the outside band and the table.

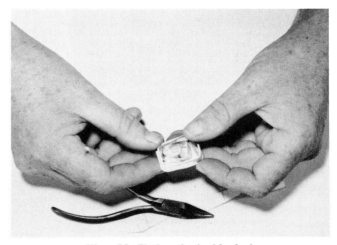

Illus. 82. Fitting the inside design.

Illus. 83. Flux all ring parts, fit them together, and place the ring on the charcoal block.

Illus. 84. After soldering, trim the inside design with the saw.

Flux all parts to be soldered, fit them together and place them on the charcoal block. Pin the work down with L-shaped wires as shown in Illus. 83.

Use *medium* solder, being sure that the pieces touch the design as well as the bottom of the table. Solder, pickle and rinse. Trim in bench vice as shown in Illus. 84.

Some filing should be needed where you joined the table and outside band (Illus. 85). When you have completed that, lay a piece of emery paper face *up* on the table and rub the sides of the ring on it until all of the file marks have disappeared.

NOTE: *Do not file the ring on top yet.* It is much easier to handle after you have attached the ring band.

Saw out the ring band next from 18-gauge silver. File the ends carefully and finish with emery paper. Bend the band using the method you learned in the first chapter (see Illus. 42). Leave a gap at the ends of the band about $\frac{1}{8}$ inch wide.

To file the sides of the ring band, hold the band firmly in your left hand. File both sides at once with the flat 6-inch file. Start at the bottom of the band and make one sweep with the file all the way to the top. After you have filed the band evenly, run the file a few times round both edges to remove the sharpness and make the band more comfortable to wear. Remove all file marks with emery paper. Next, file the two ends of the band flat until they are very thin on the inside edges (see Illus. 86).

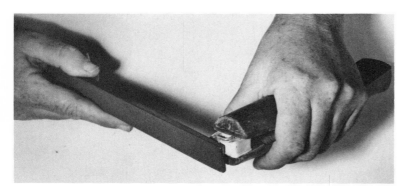

Illus. 85. File the joint of the table and the outside band.

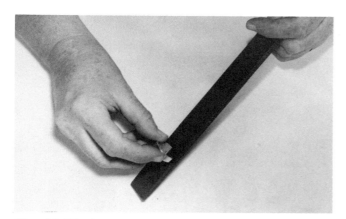

Illus. 86. File the two ends of the band until they are very thin on the inside edges.

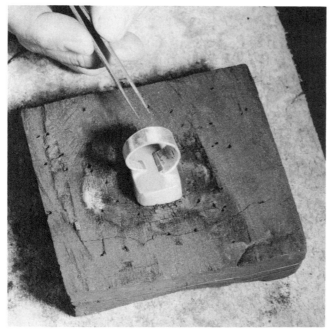

Illus. 87. Ring band ready for soldering.

place in position (see Illus. 87). Solder, pickle and rinse.

It is now time to file the ring top. Place the ring in the ring clamp. Again, use the flat 6-inch file and follow the contour of the design. Keep filing until the top is completely level (see Illus. 88).

Polish as described on pages 29 to 33. See Illus. 89 for the finished ring.

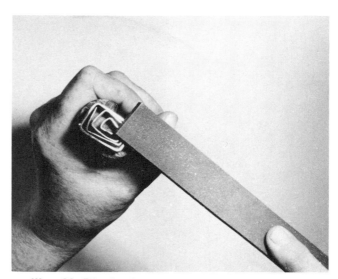

Illus. 88. File the ring top until it is completely level.

Illus. 89. The finished table ring.

When this is finished, the band is ready for soldering.

Place the table design face *down*, on the charcoal block after fluxing. Flux the band, including the flattened ends, and stand it on the bottom of the table in the proper position. Cut two thin strips of *easy* solder just long enough to cover the ends of the band. Flux and

MORE TABLE RINGS

Illus. 90. Another possible table ring which you can construct.

Now that you know the basic techniques for making a table ring, you can attempt to construct others which require much more patience and skill. The ring in Illus. 90 is one possibility.

Cut the outside band and design, following the pattern in Illus. 91, from 22-gauge silver. Once more, use the pattern for the outside band as a guide for bending. When you have completed this to your satisfaction, solder (use *hard* solder for the entire construction), pickle and rinse the band.

The next step is to inset the four bars of the design—pieces A, B, C and D. (Remember to pickle and rinse the design after each soldering.) Fit and solder bar A first. File the high butt end of the bar on a slant so the joint will be smooth and unbroken in appearance. Now fit and solder bar B. Again slant the butt ends of the bar as much as necessary for a smooth joint. Follow the same procedures for bars C and D. When you have completed this, as shown in Illus. 93, file the bottom of the design so that it is smooth and ready to be soldered to the table piece.

Scribe the outline of the design of the table

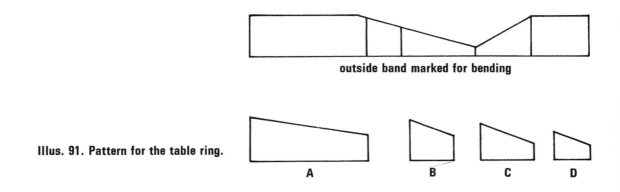

outside band marked for bending

Illus. 91. Pattern for the table ring.

A   B   C   D

on 18-gauge silver and cut it out. Set up the ring on the charcoal block and join the two pieces together with *medium* solder (see Illus. 94).

You apply the band after you have trimmed and filed the table. To do so, turn the table upside down on the charcoal block. Because of the unusual contour of the design, you have to prop up one corner of the table in order to make it level. A small piece of charcoal serves this purpose very well. Prepare the band as previously described (see page 40) and attach with *easy* solder. Now file the ring top.

Follow all of the steps for finishing the ring. The finished ring is shown in Illus. 90.

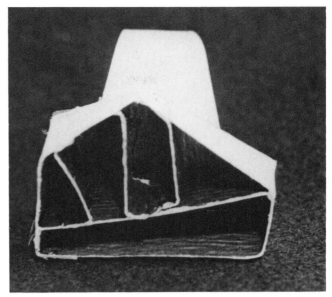

Illus. 92. Paper mock-up of the table ring in Illus. 90.

Illus. 93 (right). Design after the four bands have been soldered inside the outside band.

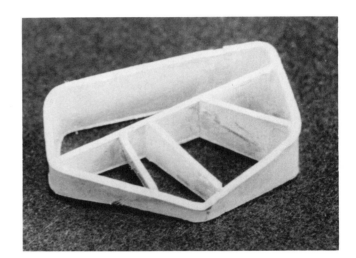

Illus. 94. Design and table after soldering.

Illus. 95 (right). Ring with the band attached, after pickling.

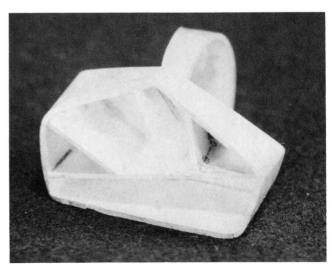

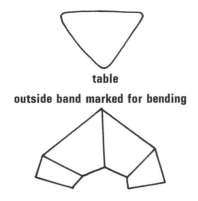

table

outside band marked for bending

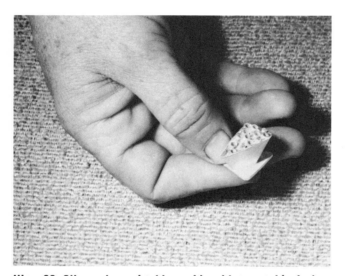

Illus. 96. Pattern for the table ring in Illus. 100.

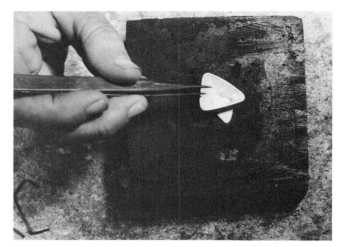

Illus. 97. Solder the outside design to the table.

Illus. 98. Silver wire and tubing soldered into outside design.

Using Silver Tubing

For the third table ring, you need a small length of 8-gauge heavy wall sterling silver tubing and a small length of 9-gauge sterling silver wire. The pattern is shown in Illus. 96. Construct the design in the same manner as the other table rings. Make the outside band of 22-gauge silver and the table and ring band of 18-gauge. Attach the outside band to the table top (Illus. 97), and then add the tubing and wire to the design.

Starting at the high end of the design, mark and cut the tube lengths so they protrude a little over the top edge of the outside band. Intersperse the pieces of tubing with lengths of silver wire. Be careful not to use too much wire as it adds weight to the total design. Solder, pickle and rinse (see Illus. 98).

When you construct any piece of jewelry with so many complicated little pieces of silver, such as this one, it is not possible to guarantee that you have rinsed all of the pickling solution out of all the little openings. It is therefore suggested that you boil the work for 10

Illus. 99. Table top and band ready for soldering, with the table propped up so it is level.

Illus. 100. Finished table ring with silver wire and tubing as part of the design.

Illus. 101. Outside band and ring band after soldering.

minutes in a solution of water and three tablespoons of baking soda to neutralize any remaining acid.

Turn the table top upside down on the charcoal block. Prop it up to make it level (see Illus. 99). Attach the band with *easy* solder. Boil in the baking soda solution once more.

Finish the ring by filing and polishing as usual. This will be much easier if you employ a ring clamp to hold the work. The finished ring is shown in Illus. 100.

Versatile Rings

Because of its versatility, the ring design in Illus. 101 is one that you should keep in your permanent files. See Illus. 102 for the pattern.

Make this ring by following the basic instructions from previous rings. By adding a little wire and simple cut-out letters, you can make this a signet ring (see Illus. 104).

In later chapters, there are instructions on flint casting and pasta throws. You may also

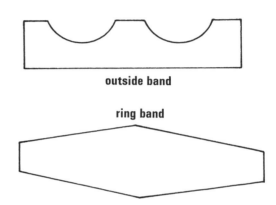

outside band

ring band

Illus. 102. Versatile pattern for a table ring.

Illus. 103. Outside band and ring band bound together on charcoal block.

Illus. 104. Finished signet ring.

Illus. 106. Another attractive ring you can make utilizes lengths of silver tubing topped by balls of shot.

Illus. 105. Stacks of silver pieces soldered together create an interesting effect.

use these techniques to create settings for this ring design.

The ring in Illus. 105 gives the effect of stacked pieces of silver. Making it is a good exercise for soldering techniques.

Another unusual ring is shown in Illus. 106. The interesting aspect of this ring is the addition of eight lengths of silver tubing, each supporting a silver ball.

BOX RING

A box ring gives the feeling of mass, without weight. It is a good construction to employ for large and fancy cocktail rings. Before you attempt this project, note that any shortcomings in the skills and techniques that you have learned up to this point will quickly be evident, for you must be very precise in the sawing, assembly and soldering processes. The design chosen for demonstration is a cocktail ring for the little finger.

Make the paper pattern for this ring, in duplicate, of light-weight cardboard (see Illus. 107). Trace the pattern for the side pieces on the cardboard. Trace the hole for the finger one size larger than the normal ring size, to allow for the insertion of the inside band. To obtain a near-perfect circle and to find the correct ring size, use a plastic circle template, which is very inexpensive and is available in any store that sells school supplies (see Illus. 108). Use the template to trace the proper ring size (see Illus. 109).

Cut the side patterns out carefully using a sharp posterboard knife, as shown in Illus. 110.

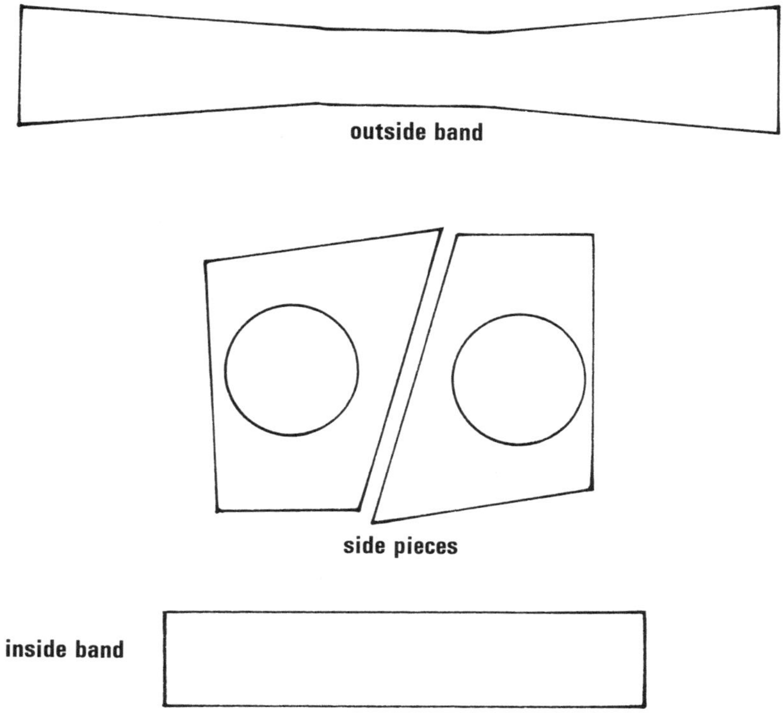

Illus. 107. Pattern for the box ring.

outside band

side pieces

inside band

Illus. 108. Use a plastic template so you can draw a near-perfect circle of the proper ring size.

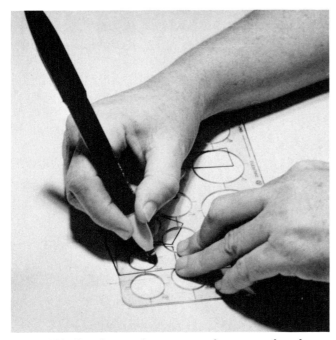

Illus. 109. Use the template to trace the correct ring size.

the measurement. When the fit is accurate, mark the duplicate pattern and trim it to the proper length. Insert the band into the circles once more with the band joint on top. Spread the two side pieces apart on the band. The top

Illus. 110. Cut out the pattern from light-weight cardboard using a posterboard knife.

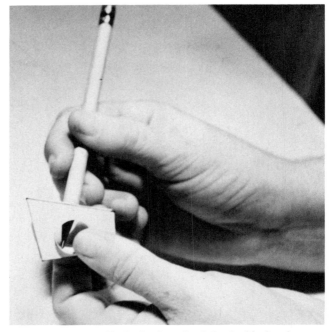

Illus. 111. Mark the length of the inside band.

For the inside band, measure and cut a strip $2\frac{1}{2}$ inches long by $\frac{1}{2}$ inch wide. Wrap the band pattern around a pencil to round it. Slip the band into the circles in the side patterns. Work with the band until it forms a perfect inside circle; then mark it for length with a pencil, as shown in Illus. 111. Remove the band and trim it to the proper length. Re-fit it to check on

50

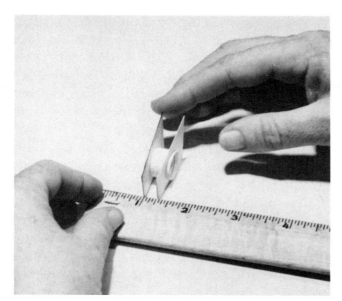

Illus. 112. Taper in the bottom side pieces so they measure $\frac{1}{4}$ inch from one outside edge to the other.

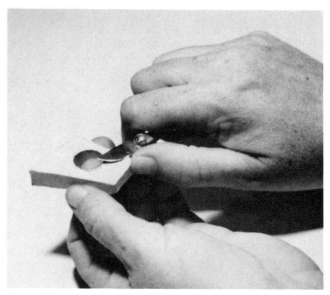

Illus. 113. Glue the outside band in place, then trim it with a posterboard knife.

of each side should be right at the edge of the band but not overlapping. The bottom of the sides should be tapered in, so that they measure $\frac{1}{4}$ inch from one outside edge to the other (see Illus. 112).

When the parts are in proper position, glue and let dry. Trim with a posterboard knife.

Trace and cut the outside band. (Note that the outside band of this ring only covers three sides, since a wooden inset fits into the fourth.) Bend it to fit the outside of the assembled parts and glue it in place. Allow it to dry and trim it with a knife (see Illus. 113 and 114).

Scribe the side piece outlines on a piece of

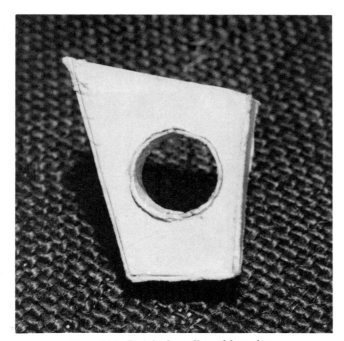

Illus. 114. Finished cardboard box ring.

Illus. 115. Scribe the ring finger holes using the template.

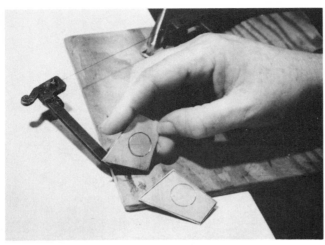

Illus. 116. Cut out the side pieces, being careful not to go over the scribed lines.

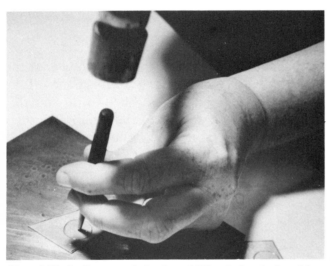

Illus. 117. Strike a mark in the middle of the circle with a punch and a hammer.

Illus. 118 (right). Start drilling in the punch mark, which keeps the drill from skidding.

18-gauge silver using the duplicate pattern. Mark the outline of the ring finger holes with a soft pencil. Remove the pattern and, using the pencilled marks as a guide for the template, scribe the lines (see Illus. 115). Cut out the side pieces, being careful not to cross over the scribed line (see Illus. 116).

Place one ring side, scribed circle up, on a steel or hardwood block. Strike a mark in the middle of the circle with a punch and hammer as illustrated in Illus. 117. Fasten the side piece to the bench pin with a small C-clamp. Place the tip of the drill on the punch mark and drill a hole (see Illus. 118). The punch mark keeps the drill from skidding and marring the surface of the silver.

When you have finished drilling, remove the ring side from the C-clamp. Loosen the top clamp on the saw frame and pull the loose end of the blade through the drilled hole (see Illus. 119).

Fasten the saw blade again. Begin to saw in a circular pattern towards the scribed line. Take great care to stay as close to the line as possible without allowing the saw cut to cross over it (see Illus. 120). Repeat this procedure with the remaining ring side.

When you have completed sawing, place the ring sides, one at a time, in the bench vice, so that the scribed circle is visible in its entirety.

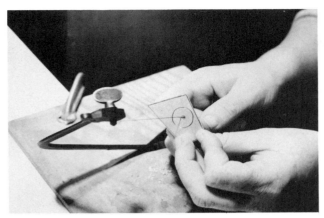

Illus. 119. Insert the saw blade through the drilled hole.

Illus. 120. Begin to saw in a circle towards the scribed line.

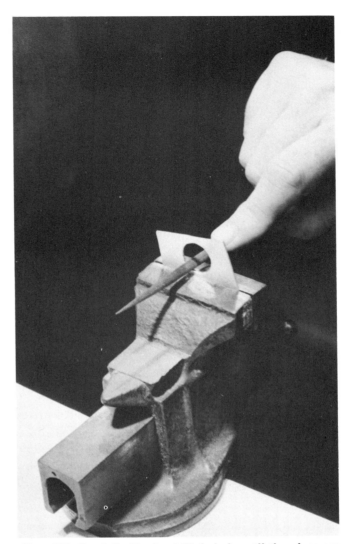

Illus. 121. Carefully file the drilled circle until the edges are even with the scribed lines.

Illus. 122. File the tops of the side pieces until they are even with the scribed marks.

File carefully until the circle is even with the scribe mark (see Illus. 121).

Match the ring sides together and place them both in the bench vice. Smooth out any irregularities which may appear in the circles with a file. Being very careful to match the circles exactly, move the ring sides down in the bench vice to ¼ inch from the top of the ring. File the tops until they are even with the scribe marks (see Illus. 122).

Lay the pattern for the inside band on a piece of 22-gauge silver and scribe the outline. Make it a little longer than the actual measurement to allow for adjustment. Saw on the outside of the scribe marks. *Do not file the band yet*. Bend the band into a circle using the forming block. True up the circle on the

Illus. 123. Fit the inside band so that it slips into the circles on the side pieces.

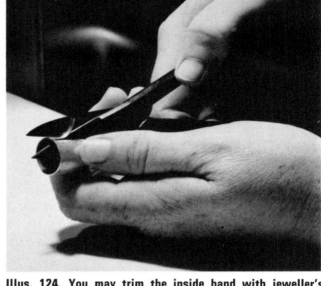

Illus. 124. You may trim the inside band with jeweller's shears if necessary.

ring mandrel. Bend the band so that the ends overlap and slip into the circles (Illus. 123).

Place the project on the ring mandrel forcing the band as high as it will go. Estimate the trim by marking the overlap with a pencil. Trim excess *a little at a time* and re-fit frequently. You may trim with jeweller's shears

Illus. 125. Ring on charcoal block ready for solder placement.

as in Illus. 124. Reverse the project on the mandrel often.

When you have achieved a good fit, lightly file the ends of the band where they join together. Clean all parts to be soldered with medium emery paper.

Assemble the parts in the proper position for soldering, with the band joint at the top center of the ring. Flux the entire project and place it on the charcoal block upside down (standing on the ring top), as shown in Illus. 125.

Since this project requires several solderings, use *hard* solder on this first step as it has the highest melting point. Clean and cut several pieces of hard solder ($\frac{1}{8}$ inch squares) and with a brush or tweezers, flux and stand the pieces on the edge of the band, leaning against the side pieces. Do this across the top on both sides of the ring. Repeat this step on the inside of the ring. Cut one piece of solder $\frac{1}{8}$ inch wide and long enough to cover the band joint, flux and place in position (see Illus. 126).

Heat the work slowly with a soft flame from the torch until the flux starts to dry. If you hurry this step, the flux will boil and cause the solder squares to jump out of place. If this

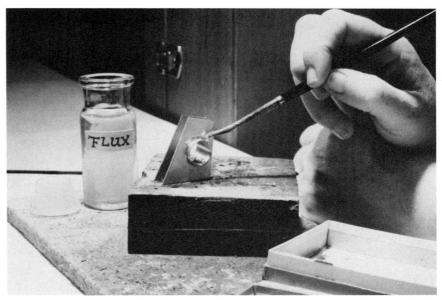

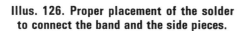
Illus. 126. Proper placement of the solder to connect the band and the side pieces.

occurs, re-flux the solder and return the squares to their proper position.

When the flux is dry, turn the torch up to a medium flame and, with a rotating motion, heat all parts of the work uniformly. Remember that hard solder has a higher melting point (1,475°F or 801°C), so that the whole heating process will take longer. As the solder melts, a bright silver line will begin to run down the circle joint. With the torch, draw the solder to the areas desired. Pickle and rinse the ring. Check very carefully for any unsoldered areas. Re-solder any areas necessary (see Illus. 127).

Trim off the excess of the inside band from both sides of the ring with the jeweller's saw (see Illus. 128). Be very careful that the saw blade does not cut into the side piece and mar it.

Illus. 127. Solder carefully, and re-solder if necessary.

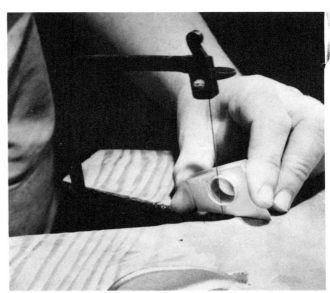
Illus. 128. Trim any excess from the inside band with the jeweller's saw.

Illus. 129. File the ring on its side on a flat file.

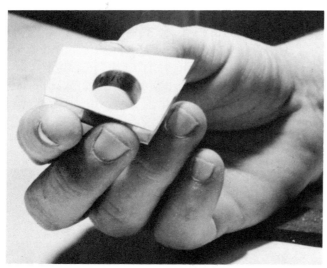

Illus. 130. File until the edge is flush, and all traces of the inside band are gone.

Lay the ring on its side on a flat file. Holding the ring securely, move it back and forth across the entire cutting surface of the file, as shown in Illus. 129. Continue filing until all traces of the edge of the inside band are gone and the entire surface is flush (see Illus. 130). Repeat on the other side of the ring. Now do all the outside edges of the ring using the same technique

with the file (see Illus. 131). Check scribe marks frequently to be sure filing is uniform.

Fit the duplicate paper pattern for the outside band to the ring parts just completed. The pattern should overlap the ring by $\frac{1}{16}$ inch

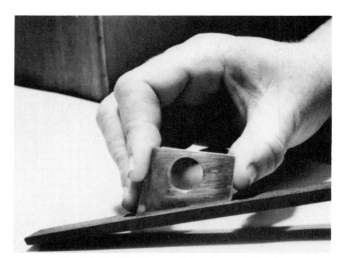

Illus. 131. File the outside edges of the ring.

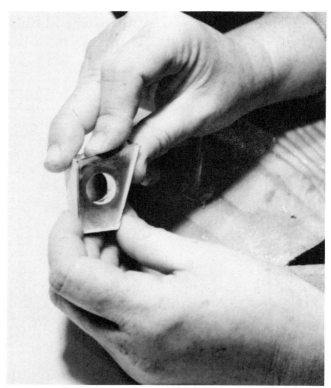

Illus. 132. Fit the paper pattern for the outside band around the parts you have already completed.

on each side and end (see Illus. 132). Make any adjustments necessary to ensure this.

Scribe and cut the outside band using 22-gauge silver. *Do not file at this point.* Bend the band to fit the ring. The corners should be sharp and as close to the contour of the ring as possible. You may use flat-nosed pliers for this purpose (see Illus. 133). If the band does not fit properly after bending, re-do it. First straighten it with your fingers, then place it on the steel block. Tap it lightly with a hammer on both sides until all traces of the bend are gone. Do not strike the silver so hard that you mar or stretch it. Anneal the band. It should now be soft enough to bend once more.

Flux all surfaces of the ring parts. Medium solder is usually used for the second soldering on any project as it has a lower melting point (1,390°F or 756°C) than hard solder. Cut several squares of medium solder $\frac{1}{16}$ inch long. Flux and place them on the inside edges of both ring sides, as in Illus. 134. Fit the outside band (Illus. 135) and bind it to the ring with binding wire (Illus. 136).

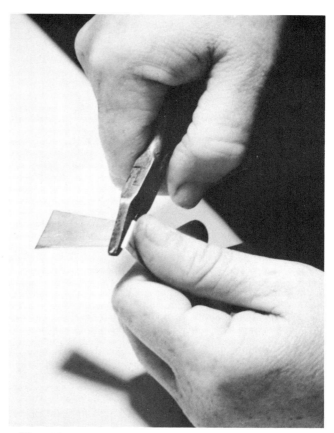

Illus. 133. Bend the outside band with flat-nosed pliers.

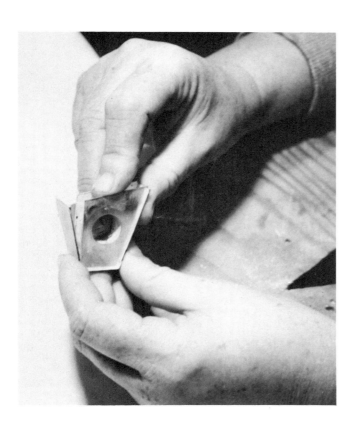

Illus. 134. Proper solder placement for the outside band.

Illus. 135 (left). Fit the outside band.

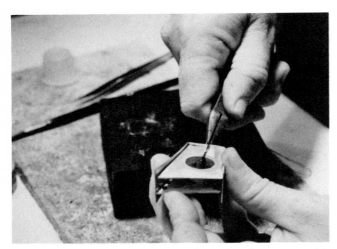

Illus. 136. Bind the outside band to the ring parts with binding wire.

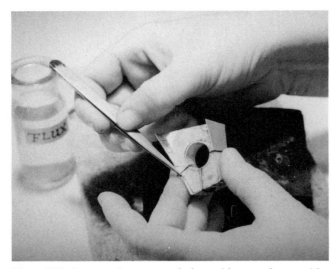

Illus. 137. Proper placement of the solder on the outside, touching the side pieces.

Place fluxed squares of *medium* solder leaning against the outside band and touching the side pieces (Illus. 137). Using a soft flame, heat the ring slowly until the flux is dry. Turn the torch up to a medium flame and heat the entire ring. Heat all parts of the ring uniformly to ensure a good soldering.

It is best to stand while soldering this part of the ring. This enables you to see all the areas you are soldering and gives greater mobility for the torch so you may heat all sides of the work uniformly. When the solder begins to melt, quickly draw it to the areas you deem necessary. Move the charcoal block and make sure all the solder has melted in all areas.

Remove all traces of the binding wire from the ring. Pickle and *rinse* thoroughly. Check the soldered areas carefully for any imperfections. Re-solder if necessary.

Lay the ring on its side on the medium flat file and move it back and forth across the entire cutting surface of the file. Follow this procedure until you have removed all traces of the outside band and the surfaces of both sides are smooth (see Illus. 139).

Very carefully file the *outside* band surfaces of the ring, remembering that the silver used for the band is much thinner than that used for the side pieces (see Illus. 140). If you fit the band correctly, very little filing is necessary.

Illus. 138. The ring is ready to be soldered.

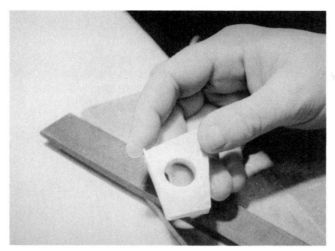

Illus. 139. Lay the ring on a medium flat file and move it back and forth.

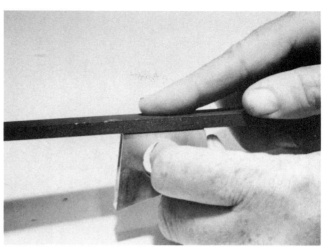

Illus. 140. Carefully file the outside edges of the ring.

Only file on this part of the ring to sharpen the design and to remove any small imperfections which may have appeared.

Now, lay the ring flat on a sheet of fine emery paper and polish all surfaces, moving the ring in one direction only (see Illus. 141). Repeat this step using a piece of extra fine emery paper. Holding the ring firmly, polish the inside band with an emery dowel (see Illus. 142). Be careful not to let the dowel dip

at either end. Follow the polishing steps as previously outlined *up to* the use of tripoli.

Now, cut and fit a piece of hardwood or bone to insert into the top of the ring. The inset in the finished ring, Illus. 145, is a piece of Brazilian Rosewood. However, you may use any hardwood. Most hardwoods are very dense and you can work with them in much the same way that you work with metal.

Lay the duplicate pattern of the ring side

Illus. 141. Use emery paper to remove any file marks.

Illus. 142. Polish the inside of the ring using the emery dowel.

Illus. 143. Lay the pattern of the ring side on the wood, and then trace, in pencil, the top one third of the pattern.

on the end of a slab of hardwood so you may outline in pencil the top one third of the pattern (see Illus. 143). Remove the pattern, and using a ruler, extend the pencilled outline on each side by $\frac{1}{2}$ inch. Using a jeweller's saw, cut out the wood insert. Now shape the wood to fit the ring by filing and sanding with emery paper.

Take a side view of the silver ring in its incomplete stage at present. Note that the ring tapers at the bottom. You must also taper the wood so it will insert into the ring.

When you have shaped the hardwood so it fits snugly, decide how high above the top of the ring you want the wood to extend. The height of the wood in the example, Illus. 144, is $\frac{1}{8}$ inch. Cut the wood to the desired height. Sand the top of the inset on a piece of medium emery paper. Repeat, using a piece of fine emery paper. Also polish, with the fine emery paper, all surfaces of the wood that are to be exposed.

Coat the bottom of the insert liberally with white glue. Fit it into the ring and let it set until dry. Then polish the wood with a neutral wax, such as shoe wax, or by using white rouge on a clean polishing stick.

Illus. 145 shows the finished ring.

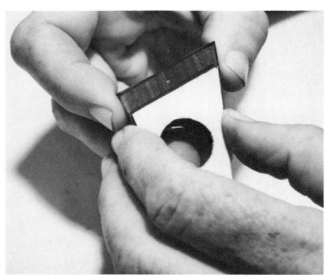

Illus. 144. Determine the height you want the wood inset to be.

Illus. 145. The finished box ring is certainly attractive.

PENDANTS

The construction of pendants, such as the first one in this chapter (see the pattern in Illus. 146), is much the same as the construction of a table top ring. The first step is, as always, the mock-up (see Illus. 147).

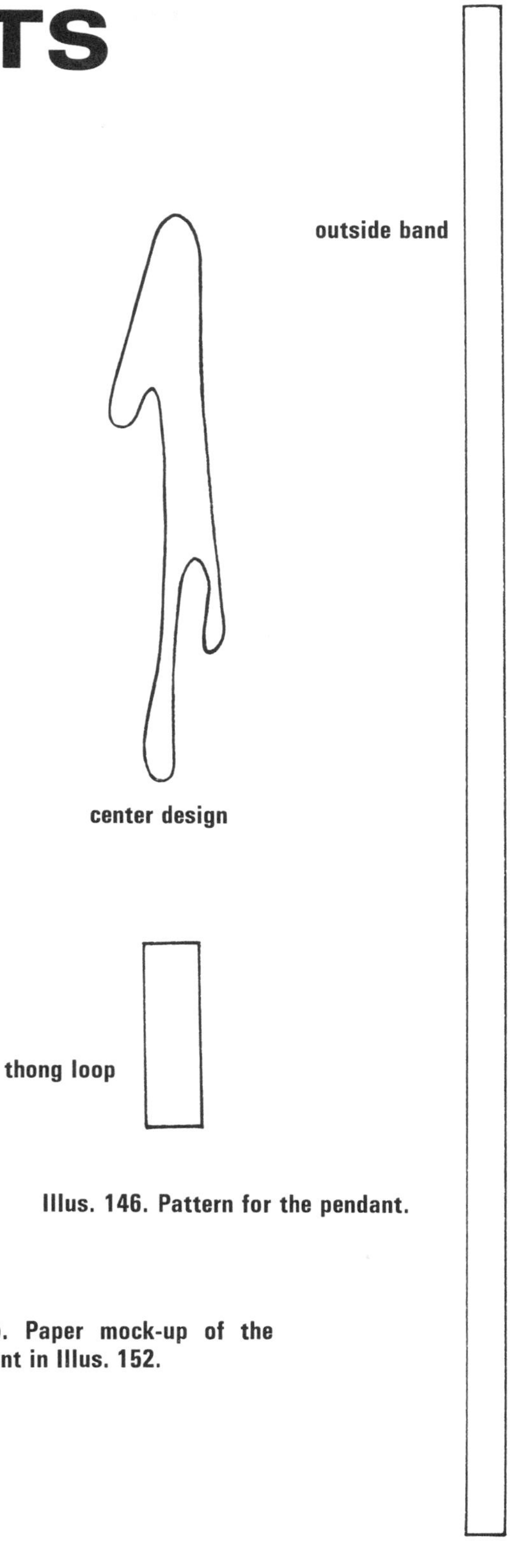

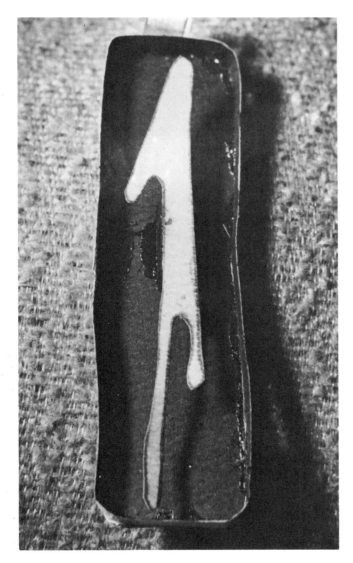

outside band

center design

thong loop

Illus. 146. Pattern for the pendant.

Illus. 147 (left). Paper mock-up of the pendant in Illus. 152.

Illus. 148. The outside band is pinned to the charcoal block.

Note that the middle of the design in this pendant is elevated from the floor of the pendant with two silver blocks. The outside band is made of 18-gauge silver. Because of the length, it is necessary to piece this band on the side and away from where it will be bent. The design and floor of the pendant are made of 22-gauge silver.

Saw out the parts as usual. Bend the outside band using the paper pattern as a guide. Solder, pickle and rinse. Use the soldered outside band as a guide for scribing the floor of the pendant.

Ready the parts for soldering and then, use four L-shaped pins to fasten them to the charcoal block as shown in Illus. 149. NOTE: Use *hard* solder on this step. Lean the snippets against the side so they touch the bottom of the pendant. Solder, pickle and rinse.

Prepare the middle design for soldering. Take special care in finishing this part as it is the focal point of the pendant. Cut four pieces of 18-gauge silver $\frac{1}{2}$ inch long and $\frac{1}{16}$ inch wide. You do not have to finish these pieces as they block up the middle design. Prepare them for soldering and join them together, using *hard* solder, to form two silver blocks (Illus. 150). Pickle and rinse.

Illus. 149. The pendant parts are ready to be soldered, pinned to the charcoal block.

Illus. 150. The two silver blocks are ready for soldering.

Use the middle design as a guide and position the silver blocks in a spot that gives the most support to it. Mark the spot with the scribe and remove the block. Flux everything thoroughly. Place two pieces of *medium* solder on each end of the marked spot. Place the block on top of this. Dry the flux slowly with a soft flame so the block does not jump out of place. Solder, pickle and rinse.

Cut a strip of 18-gauge silver, one inch long and ¼ inch wide, for the thong loop. File the ends so they are smooth. Using round-nose pliers, bend it into a circle. Place this in the bench vice and file the two ends flat. File both sides of the circle. Remove all file marks with emery paper. Prepare the thong for soldering.

Use *easy* solder for the middle design. Flux all parts thoroughly. Place three fluxed snippets of solder on each block that will support the middle design. Dry the flux with a soft flame. Position the design and pin it to the charcoal block.

Illus. 151. The thong loop is ready for soldering.

Illus. 152 (above). Attach a leather thong or other hanging device to complete your pendant.

Dig a small hole in the charcoal block at the end where you will solder the thong loop to help support and center it. The loop should fit snugly against the outside band. Cut a piece of solder as wide as the loop and place it on top of the loop where it will join. Dry the flux with a soft flame. Solder, pickle and rinse. Then follow the procedures for polishing to finish your first pendant.

Illus. 153. Close-up of the finished pendant for detail.

Other Ideas for Pendants

The pendant shown in Illus. 156 is tricky because you must bend the outside band at very sharp angles. Piece the outside band on the slightly curved side of the design. Do all finish filing before you solder the oval design in place.

Prop up the oval design, which rests on top of the line inset, from the underside with a silver block.

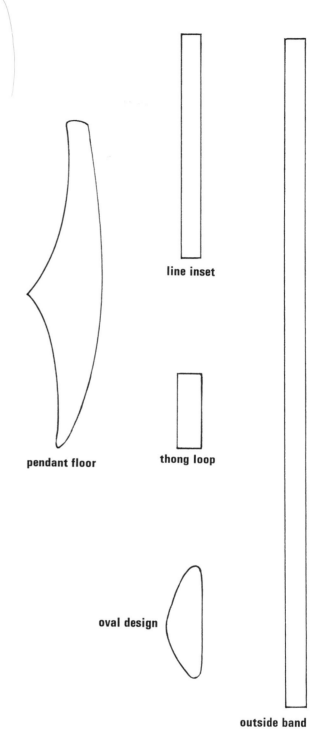

line inset

pendant floor

thong loop

oval design

outside band

Illus. 155. Pattern for the pendant shown in Illus. 156.

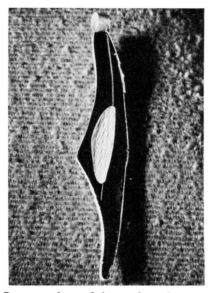

Illus. 154. Paper mock-up of the pendant shown in Illus. 156.

Illus. 156 (left). Finished pendant.

Illus. 157. Close-up of the pendant in Illus. 156.

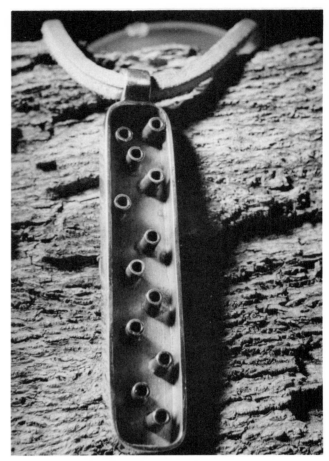

Illus. 158. Simply solder lengths of silver tubing to the floor of a pendant to create this effect.

Illus. 159. Silver tubing, soldered to the floor of a pendant and topped with shot balls, created this unique pendant.

The third pendant, shown in Illus. 158, is an exercise in effect. To make this pendant, cut lengths of silver tubing and then solder them to the floor of the pendant. Upon completion of this step, file the design smooth.

For the pendant in Illus. 159, cut silver tubing in varying lengths and solder it to the floor of the pendant. When you have completed this, solder a silver ball to each piece of tubing.

FLINT CASTING

EQUIPMENT IDENTIFICATION (Illus. 160)

A: coping saw, for cutting air vents in the flint cast

B: carving tools, which you can either purchase in any ceramic supply shop or improvise by using a sharpened screwdriver or broken dental tools

C: sandpaper, to sand the tops of the flint blocks smooth

D: mixing bowl, in which you mix the plaster and flint with water

E: spoon, to mix the plaster, flint and water

F: tweezers, to handle the hot silver when necessary

G: cottage cheese or other small plastic or wooden cartons to use as moulds for the flint blocks

H: scrap silver, preferably small pieces to make melting easier

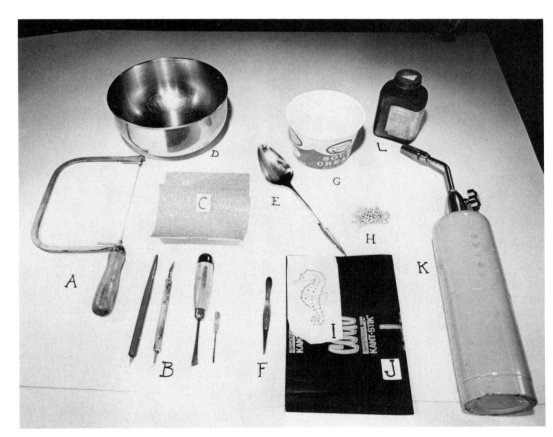

Illus. 160. Equipment for flint casting.

Illus. 161. Pattern for the flint casting in Illus. 165.

I: design you will carve, which you draw on paper

J: carbon paper, to transfer the design to the flint block

K: torch, to melt the silver

L: borax, to add to melting silver to cause all of the impurities to rise to the surface from where you can easily remove them

M: flint and plaster of Paris (not pictured), the ingredients you use to make flint casting blocks

How to Flint Cast

If the primitive, with all of its little imperfections, appeals to you, try this unusual technique.

First, make the basic formula: three parts plaster of Paris to one part of flint. Add enough water so that the mixture is just mushy enough to pour. Pour the mixture into clean cottage cheese containers. Bounce the filled containers on the work bench two or three times to bring the air bubbles to the surface. As soon as the mixture begins to set, peel the container away. If your container is wooden, you will have to break it to get the block out.

Then cure the blocks by letting them stand for two or three days or by placing them in the

Illus. 162. Transfer your chosen design, using carbon paper, to the flint-cast block.

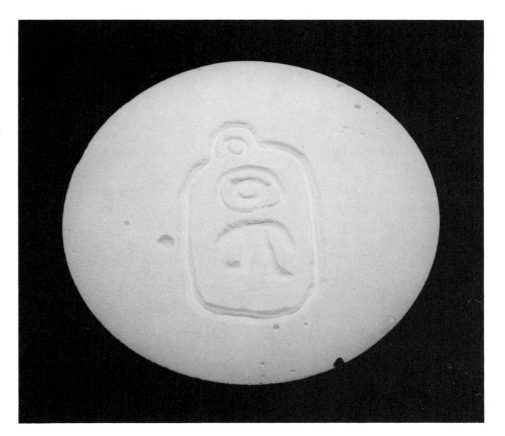

Illus. 163. Flint block after carving.

oven for four hours at 350°F (154°C). When the blocks have been cured, sand the tops flat. Do the sanding outside so you need not worry about the fine white dust that accumulates. Lay a sheet of sandpaper face up on a flat surface and sand the block by moving it back and forth. Sand until you have removed most of the surface bubbles.

Have your drawn design ready (the pattern for the design demonstrated here is shown in Illus. 161). Transfer it to the surface of the block by using carbon paper. You may use anything that works as a carving tool. Broken dental tools work well or you may sharpen a small screwdriver and use it for carving. Also, you may purchase and use regular carving tools. Use a pointed tool and first inscribe the outside outline of the design in the plaster of Paris and flint mould. Follow the lines and deepen them to about ¼ inch.

Note that the deepest parts of the carving will be the high and shiny surfaces when the casting is pulled and polished. Therefore, the outline and the thong loop of this design should be the deepest part of the carving. When the outline has reached the proper depth, slope the lines by running the carving tool along each edge. The effect of this is a V-shaped line with the narrow part at the bottom and the wide part on top.

Now carve the middle figure. Remember to slope any hard lines here too. Take special pains to make the body of the figures as smooth as possible.

Tear a small corner from a piece of sandpaper and sand what will be the floor of the design until it is all smooth. Remove dust from the casting by merely slapping it against your hand. Finish carving to your satisfaction.

Now, carve four air vents which allow air to

escape when you press the molten silver into the carving. Cut the lines for the vents to the desired depth with a coping saw. The lines should penetrate the design to its center (see Illus. 164). Once more, remember to slope the lines and make them widest at the edge of the block.

Before you do anything else, set up your work area. Place all tools so you can easily see them and can reach them without taking your eyes from the mould. Place the asbestos pad directly in front of you. Put the flint block, which you have carved, on top and in the middle of the pad. Place a pair of soldering tweezers on the asbestos pad to the left of the carving. Place the pile of scrap silver, which you will use, next to the tweezers. The borax bottle should also be on the left with the cap removed and a small spoon sticking out of it. Also, have an extra flint block on the left within easy reach.

Remember you will be dealing with molten silver so exercise great care as all objects become very hot during this process.

Melt the scrap silver with the torch, a little at a time on top of the carving. Do not remove the flame from the melting silver as it cools quickly. Add one or two small scraps of silver at a time. Be sure they are thoroughly melted before adding more. When you have enough melted silver to equal the size of a quarter (a circle about an inch in diameter) on the block, add borax. Do not add too much, just enough to cover the tip of the spoon. When the mass of silver covers two thirds of the carving, add another small amount of borax.

Now reach for the spare block and have it ready in your hand. Remove the flame of the torch and press the block on top of the silver mass. Remove the pressing block and inspect the casting. If it has not completely covered the design, re-heat the silver until it becomes

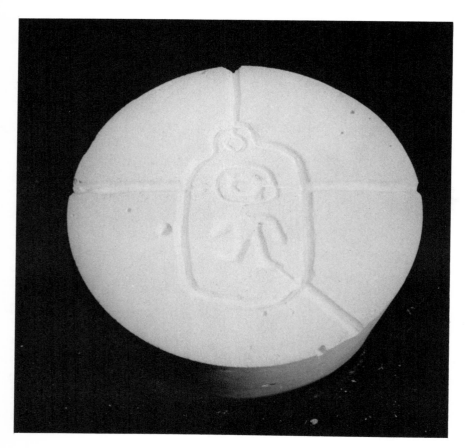

Illus. 164. Flint block after air vents have been carved.

Illus. 165. Finished flint-cast pendant.

soft enough to move once more. You must play the torch over the entire mass so it becomes evenly heated. Add more silver if necessary. Press again.

Pry the casting loose from the mould with the tweezers. Remember that everything is hot. Quench the casting in water. Clean flint away from the face of the casting with a small pick, a toothbrush and water. Trim the casting with the jeweller's saw.

Fasten the project to the bench pin with a small C-clamp and drill the hole for the thong loop (see page 34 for drilling instructions). Pickle and rinse. Remove the air vent marks with a small file and finish file the entire object. Oxidize and polish using the usual procedures.

Illus. 165 shows the finished casting.

Abstract Pendant

The second little pendant, whose pattern is shown in Illus. 166, is cast the same way as the first. Illus. 167 shows the carving with air vents. Illus. 168 is the silver after it has been pressed

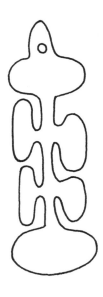

Illus. 166. Pattern for the abstract pendant.

71

into the mould. Note the pressing block. In Illus. 169, the cast pendant has just been pried out of the mould. Illus. 170 is the pendant after cleaning and pickling, and Illus. 171 is the finished pendant.

Illus. 167 (left). Flint block after air vents have been carved.

Illus. 168 (right). The silver has been pressed into the carved mould.

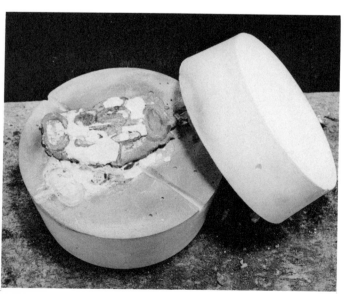

Illus. 169 (left). The casting has been pried from the mould.

Illus. 170. Casting after pickling.

Illus. 171. Finished pendant. Use this design, or create any one you especially like.

Illus. 172. Close-up of the pendant for detail.

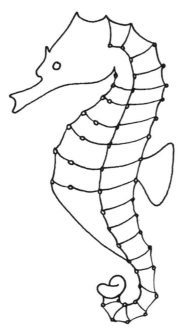

Illus. 173. Pattern for the seahorse pendant.

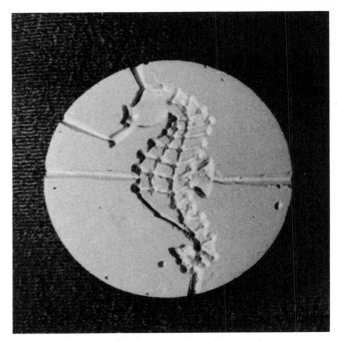

Illus. 174. Seahorse design after carving.

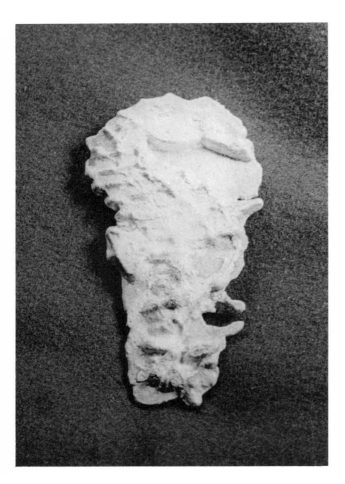

Seahorse Pendant

The last flint cast design whose pattern is shown in Illus. 173, is the most difficult and you should only attempt it after much practice with this process. It requires the use of two propane torches (but only one if you are using an oxygen and gas torch) because of the size of the design and the amount of silver you will melt. Also, take great care with the carving, remembering to slope all of the lines (see Illus. 174).

Begin to melt the silver in the usual way. When the mass reaches the point where it becomes difficult to melt, have someone light the second torch and heat the side of the mass furthest from you. When you are ready to press the silver into the mould, alert the person helping you to remove the flame of their

Illus. 175. The seahorse casting after pickling.

torch on your command. It may take several pressings to complete the cast. Be patient as the melting of this much silver does take time. Remove the cast and finish in the usual way.

Solder a small ring on the top of the design as a thong or chain loop. Illus. 176 shows the finished seahorse.

Rings for Keys and Fingers

You can find a variety of design ideas in any book on fossil identification or primitive designs. Some of these little figures lend themselves very well to key chain ornaments (or pendants, of course). See, for instance, Illus. 177 and 178.

A simple carving can also, with the addition of a band, give you a nice little ring (see Illus. 179 and 180).

Follow the techniques you have learned to make these unique gift items.

Illus. 176. Finished seahorse pendant.

Illus. 177. This is one simple design you can use to decorate a key ring.

Illus. 178. This simple design lends itself well to a key chain.

Illus. 179. A simple carving makes an effective flint-cast ring.

Illus. 180. Draw an abstract design or other pattern, and make a flint casting of it to mount on a ring.

PASTA THROW

EQUIPMENT (Illus. 181)
A: spaghetti
B: borax
C: torch
D: charcoal block and asbestos pad

E: stainless steel bowl
F: tweezers
G: scrap silver

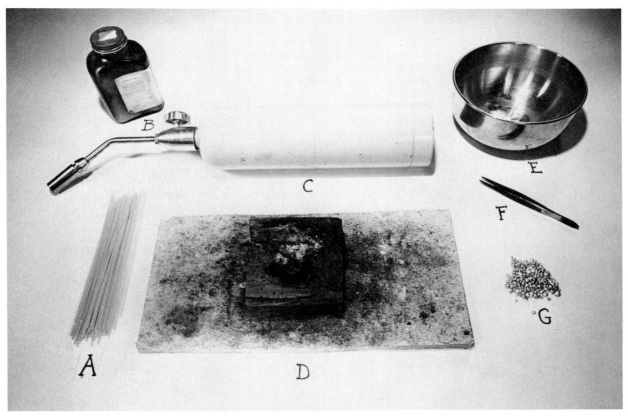

Illus. 181. Pasta-throw equipment.

Illus. 182. Remove the silver pieces from the spaghetti with tweezers.

This is a bit of accidental art which you may incorporate with the ring-making techniques which you have already learned.

Boil a handful of spaghetti in the stainless bowl for 10 minutes. Pour all but 2 inches of water from the bowl and place it on the asbestos pad. Dig a little hollow in the charcoal block and melt some silver scraps, adding a small amount of borax when the silver is molten.

Very carefully pick up the charcoal block keeping the flame of the torch focussed on the silver. Remove the flame and dump the silver over the spaghetti. The molten silver should conform in shape to the spaghetti you have poured it over.

Now, remove the silver pieces with the tweezers. Sometimes, with luck, you will get a handsome piece of silver that needs very little done to it to make a pendant or key chain decoration. Illus. 183 is an example of this. For the most part however, you will have to cut off the little buds and use them as settings in rings, and so on. See Illus. 184.

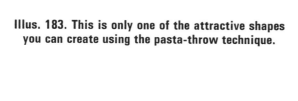

Illus. 183. This is only one of the attractive shapes you can create using the pasta-throw technique.

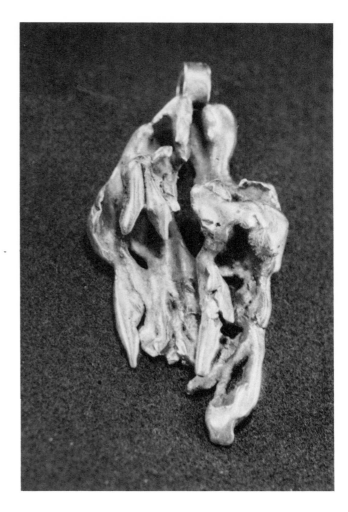

Illus. 184. Sometimes, the little silver buds that result from a pasta throw make appropriate settings for rings.

SILVER AND WOOD INLAY

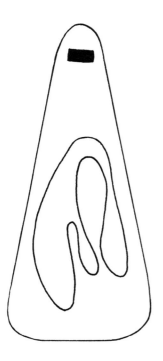

Illus. 185. Pattern for the silver and wood inlay pendant.

on the slab and trace the outline with a pencil. Use the jeweller's saw to cut it out.

Mark, with a pencil, the area you plan to cut out for the insertion of the thong loop. Fasten the pendant to the bench pin with the small C-clamp and drill a hole in the middle of the marked area. Unfasten the top of the

Illus. 186. Inlay design for the pendant after carving.

The combination of silver and wood is pleasant and attractive. This chapter instructs you in one of the most simple forms of silver and wood inlay.

Any kind of hardwood is adaptable to this type of inlay. Teak is used for the examples in this chapter. Cut the wood you plan to use into a slab $\frac{1}{4}$ inch thick. Place the design for the pendant shape (see Illus. 185 for one idea)

Illus. 187. Sand the pendant, first with sandpaper, then with emery, until the wood and the silver are level.

saw blade, slip it through the hole and fasten it once more. Saw out the area. Remove the saw blade.

Scribe the outline of the center design on a piece of 22-gauge silver and cut it out. File the design carefully and when it is finished to your liking, trace its outline on the wood with a pencil.

Fasten the pendant to the bench pin with the small C-clamp. Using a sharp carving tool, follow the outline of the design until you have made a cut all the way round it. With a flat bladed carving tool, carve a bed for the silver design. Try to achieve a uniform depth of $\frac{1}{16}$ inch. Fit the design often and whittle away unwanted wood a little at a time. Your aim is to achieve the closest fit possible.

When you have completed the fitting, place a layer of wood putty in the cavity and force the silver design down into the bed. A good tool for this is a pencil with an eraser.

Next, sand the pendant, using medium sandpaper first, going with the grain of the wood. When your sanding has almost reached the level of the silver inlay, switch to fine emery paper. Sand with the emery until the silver and wood are all at the same level and you have achieved a fine matt finish on all parts of the silver.

You may finish the wood in any of several ways. Two of the easiest methods are to rub it with linseed oil or to leave it natural. Or, you may use neutral shoe wax and then buff it to a high gloss.

Saw out the thong loop, using 18-gauge silver. File the edges and rub to a matt finish with emery. With the flat-nosed pliers, make the first bend in the thong loop. Insert the

Illus. 188. Note the special effect you can achieve with a silver inlay into a wooden pendant, as shown here.

Illus. 189. Pattern for the wood and silver pendant in Illus. 191.

silver in the hole and finish bending. See Illus. 188 for the finished pendant.

See Illus. 189 to 191 for another idea for a wood and silver pendant.

Illus. 190. Wooden pendant after it has been carved.

Illus. 191. Completed wood and silver pendant.

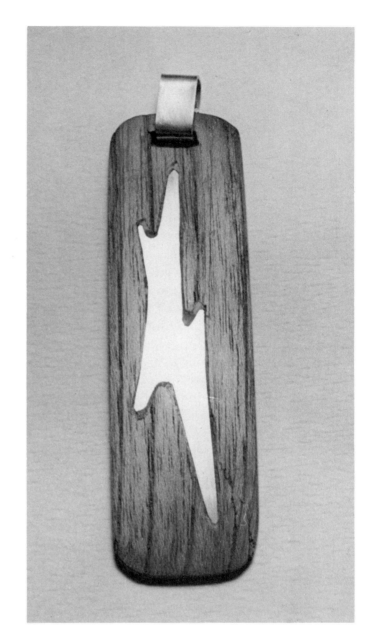

BUTTONS

The major things to remember when making buttons are size and weight. You must make buttons of light-weight silver so they will not weigh down the material to which you sew them. They must also be of a practical size, so you may use them over and over again on different articles of clothing.

The example of buttons below (in Illus. 193) are, once more, based on the principles learned in making the table ring. You construct the buttons of 22-gauge silver and silver tubing. Solder a small ring of light-weight silver to the back of each button so you may sew it to the garment.

The pair of buttons in Illus. 192, on the other hand, were flint cast. Notice that they were cast very thin to eliminate unnecessary weight.

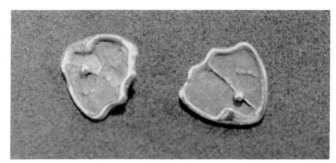

Illus. 192. Use the flint-casting technique to make personalized, handsome buttons.

NOTE: In small and uncomplicated castings, such as this, it is possible to get more than one cast from a carving if you exercise care when prying it out. Add a small ring on the back of each button.

Illus. 193. You can construct these buttons using the same techniques that you used to make a table ring.

BELT BUCKLES

Belt buckles afford you the opportunity of "thinking big" in terms of design. The two designs shown in Illus. 195 and 197 illustrate how dramatic the designs can be.

Flint-Cast Buckle

The example in Illus. 195 is a flint-cast buckle. The design (shown in Illus. 194) is an adaptation of a fossilized fish. After you have cast it, as described on pages 67 to 71, file it on

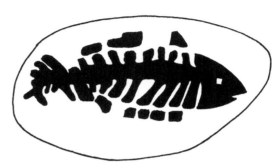

Illus. 194. Pattern for the fossilized fish flint-cast buckle.

Illus. 195. Finished flint-cast fish buckle.

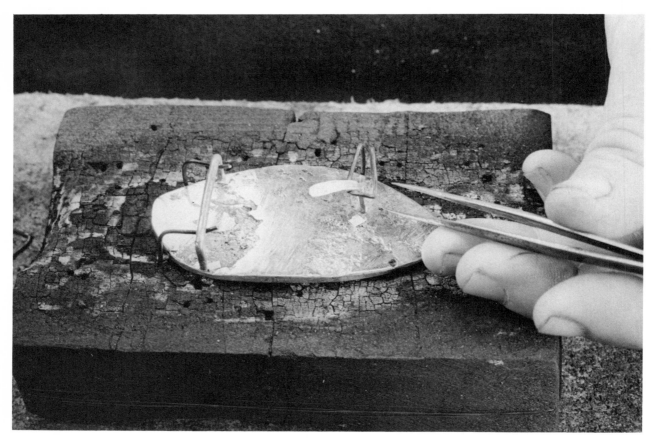

Illus. 196. Flint-cast belt buckle fastenings ready to be soldered.

the back just enough to give it a good seat for the fastenings which you will solder to it.

Cut a piece of silver wire ¾ inch long. Place the end of it on the steel block. Using the metal end of the hammer, forge it into a paddle shape. File the ends until they are smooth and uniform. Bend the wire ¼ inch from one end.

Cut another piece of silver wire 1½ inches long and file the ends. Bend the wire ¼ inch from each end to form a long U shape.

Brace the fastenings with heavy binding wire as shown in Illus. 196. Lean a snippet of medium solder against each joint. Solder, pickle and rinse. Finish in the usual way.

Sheet Silver Buckle

The belt buckle in Illus. 197 is made of 22-gauge sheet silver. (The pattern is shown in Illus. 198). Saw out Part A first, then Part B.

Each little square round the circumference of the design must have a starter hole which you should drill through it and then saw out. Finish file these little pierced areas very carefully with a needle file.

Now cut out Parts C and D and finish file. Cut the eyes, Part E, next and also pierce and finish file them. Cut out the nose, Part F (three silver wires), and prepare for soldering.

Now assemble the buckle, starting with Parts A and B. Place Part A on the charcoal block and flux. Be sure to ring the outside edge of the silver with enough snippets of hard solder to ensure a well soldered edge. Place several snippets of solder strategically in the middle of the design as well. Flux Part B thoroughly and pin the two parts together on the charcoal block.

Since the pieces of solder are not visible, in this particular instance, watch the top piece

Illus. 197. This rugged-looking buckle is an attractive addition to a sturdy leather belt.

Fashion and attach the fastenings for the buckle in the same way as on the first belt buckle (see page 86), using easy solder.

When you have completed soldering, boil the buckle for 10 minutes in a baking soda solution (refer to pages 46 to 47). Finish in the usual way.

You are now acquainted with the basics of working with silver. You are on your own to create unique rings and many other things.

carefully. When the solder melts, this top piece drops slightly. Pickle and rinse.

Follow the same procedures for soldering Parts C and D which you may do at the same time, using medium solder. Pickle and rinse. Do Parts E and F next, using easy solder. Pickle and rinse.

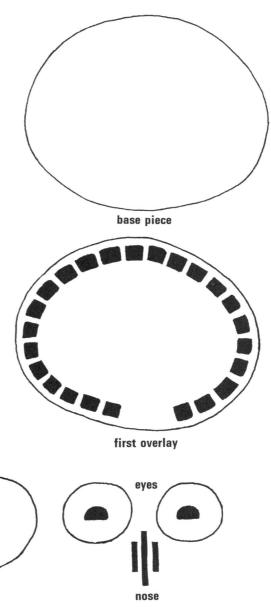

base piece

first overlay

Illus. 198. Pattern for the sheet silver belt buckle.

eyes

nose

second overlays

INDEX